# THE IDEAS AND MEDITATIVE PRACTICES OF EARLY BUDDHISM

# THE IDEAS AND MEDITATIVE PRACTICES OF EARLY BUDDHISM

BY

TILMANN VETTER

E.J. BRILL
LEIDEN • NEW YORK • KØBENHAVN • KÖLN
1988

This book was translated with the financial assistance of the Netherlands Organization for Scientific Research (NWO)

Cover design: Roel van Dijk



**Library of Congress Cataloging-in Publication-Data**

Vetter, Tilmann.
The ideas and meditative practices of early Buddhism / by Tilmann Vetter.
p. cm.
Translated from Dutch, with revisions.
Bibliography: p.
Includes index.
ISBN 90-04-08959-4 (pbk.)
1. Meditation—Buddhism. 2. Buddhism—Doctrines—History—Early period, to ca. 250 B.C. I. Title.
BQ5612.V47 1988
294.3'443—dc19 88-29318
CIP

ISBN 90 04 08959 4



PRINTED IN THE NETHERLANDS BY E. J. BRILL

CONTENTS

CONTENTS

# PREFACE

Since 1983 there have been several revisions of this book in the Dutch language. My original intention was to introduce university students to the ideas and meditative practices of early Buddhism. As I was familiar with recent literature which is highly critical of the presupposed unity of canonical tradition, I could no longer just reiterate the synthesizing interpretations handed down to us mainly from the Theravāda school. Consequently I had to evolve my own way of describing the tenets. It seemed worth the effort to bring the results of this attempt to the attention of Buddhologists outside the Netherlands by translating it into English. Compared to the last Dutch version of the book, some parts have been improved in the course of this process.

Not many details are discussed as the book is still intended to be an introduction to early Buddhism. I hope that Buddhist scholars will accept this limitation and concentrate on the main lines. I have demonstrated that things are sometimes much more complicated in a paper for the VIIth World Sanskrit Conference (Leiden August, 1987) entitled "Some remarks on older parts of the Suttanipāta" (forthcoming). It also contains my answer to the opinion that the most ancient form of Buddhism can be found in the Suttanipāta. A portion of this paper is, in a slightly adapted form and without notes, appended to this book under the title "Mysticism in the Aṭṭhakavagga".

The section in this book entitled "An Outline of the Most Ancient Form of Buddhism" tries to describe the method I applied and its results. It is the revised version of an article that has already been published under the title "Recent Research on the Most Ancient Form of Buddhism: A Possible Approach and its Results" in *Buddhism and its Relation to Other Religions. Essays in Honour of Dr. Shozen Kumoi on His Seventieth Birthday*" (Kyoto 1985, 67-85).

In this preface I should like to briefly describe my approach to Buddhist canonical texts in general. In my opinion these texts do not indubitably report the words of the Buddha and his first disciples even though they purport to be a true account. But we must also not discard the possibility that sometimes, in the nucleus of a text, the words of the Buddha may be found. If one does not accept that all the words in these texts are words of the Buddha and his disciples, it does not mean that then one accuses the authors or editors of being liars. There are, indeed, certain passages where one is inclined to use such a strong word or a milder one to describe the attribution of the contents to the Buddha. In many cases, however, the best explanation of what happened seems to be that if a particular idea had become accepted, one could scarcely imagine that it had not been preached by the Buddha himself. An interesting example of how this question could be treated is found in W. Pannenberg, Das Irreale des Glaubens, in: *Funktionen des Fiktiven* edited by D. Henrich & W. Iser, Poetik und Hermeneutik Bd. X, München 1983.

There is one point in the ancient Buddhist sermons and dialogues where a glimmering of this emerges. In Anguttara Nikāya 8.1.8 the venerable Uttara says, "It is good that a monk every now and then examines the failures of himself and others as well as the successes of himself and others". Then the god Indra appears and asks him "Is this doctrine your inspiration or is it the word of the Buddha?" Uttara does not give a direct answer. He says, "It is like a great heap of grain from which one takes a few kernels; all that has been well spoken (*subhāsitam*) is the Buddha's word".

I can also use this text to comment on the methodology I apply in approaching these sermons and dialogues which in Pāli are called *sutta* (as R. Gombrich recently observed, the term *sutta* seems to have corresponded to Sanskrit *sūkta* "well spoken", synonymous with *subhāṣita*, and to have been incorrectly translated into Sanskrit as *sūtra* some centuries later). Further on in this same sermon we read that Uttara's statement on the examination of the failures and successes of himself and others was once used by the Buddha in connection with the judgement of the monk Devadatta. It is stated that none of those present had remembered the statement except Uttara because he was given the task of preserving it. One could ask why Uttara had not related this incident to the god Indra. I can only explain this story of Uttara's preserving the text as the work of another author. Consequently I feel no obligation to take this second story into consideration when I quote the first story to illustrate the problematics of the true and false Buddha word.

We now arrive at the observation that many transmitted texts are more or less inconsistent. This holds for a single sentence, for a sermon and for the entire collection of sermons (P.*sutta-piṭaka*). This inconsistency is quite different from that of daily discourse and writing. There was respect for transmission and that is why we may assume that generally nothing was ever discarded, only perhaps forgotten. But the texts were continuously expanded. The inconsistences resulting from this are not easily discernible because they deal mainly with abstract concepts which are difficult to grasp; also an attempt at synthesis is often made. People have learned to live with inconsistencies in almost every religious tradition because they have to accept a transmission as a whole. This also holds true for Buddhists as well as most Western scholars who accepted everything as the word of the Buddha, at least when presented as such in the "sober" Pali texts. Historical research has now arrived at the stage when a large number of contradictions and deviations have clearly become apparent. Unless one takes inconsistency as a characteristic of each religious consciousness, one may look for a way out of the dilemmas by assuming a development of thought. In ancient Buddhism the structure of the separate tenets does not give any reason for proposing the first solution, i.e. accepting inconsistency as a characteristic of it.

A step towards a more acute observation of inconsistent doctrines has especially been made by L. Schmithausen in a recent article (1981). Subsequently J. Bronkhorst and others have also made some important discoveries. In the meantime the facts have become so varied that we can no longer explain everything by attributing it to a development in the thinking of the Buddha himself as E. Frauwallner (1953) tried to do. But this does not mean to imply that we should give up such an approach altogether.

It is now also evident that the method considered so trustworthy by Frauwallner and others which consists of a comparison of the different extant versions of a text (Pāli, Sanskrit, Chinese) does not just simply lead to the oldest nucleus of the doctrine. The only thing that can be established is that in this way one arrives at a Sthavira canon dating from c. 270 B.C. when the missionary activities during Asoka's reign as well as dogmatic disputes had not yet created divisions within the Sthavira tradition. But even then one is not completely certain of reaching an old canon, because the different schools exchanged tenets after this period (see G. Schopen, Two Problems in the History of Indian Buddhism, in: *Studien zur Indologie und Iranistik*, Heft 10 [1984] 9-47). I do not want to exclude the possibility that a doctrine which is not found in a common tradition could also be very ancient. But in general by uncovering a common core one does come closer to finding the oldest doctrines than when one does not use such a method. As I have already indicated whatever inconsistences do remain, one must try to unravel by using a different method. Striving to reach a common core which can then be examined for inconsistencies is an arduous task and certainly one which has not yet been completed. In this context, with due respect, I should like to mention the work of A. Bareau: *Recherches sur la Biographie du Buddha*, (since 1963).

Finally I should like to thank those people who have read parts or all of an earlier Dutch version of this book and who have commented on its contents. I am also obliged to Marianne Oort for her efforts in translating this version into English and to Lambert Schmithausen for making some suggestion to improve the contents of the English version.

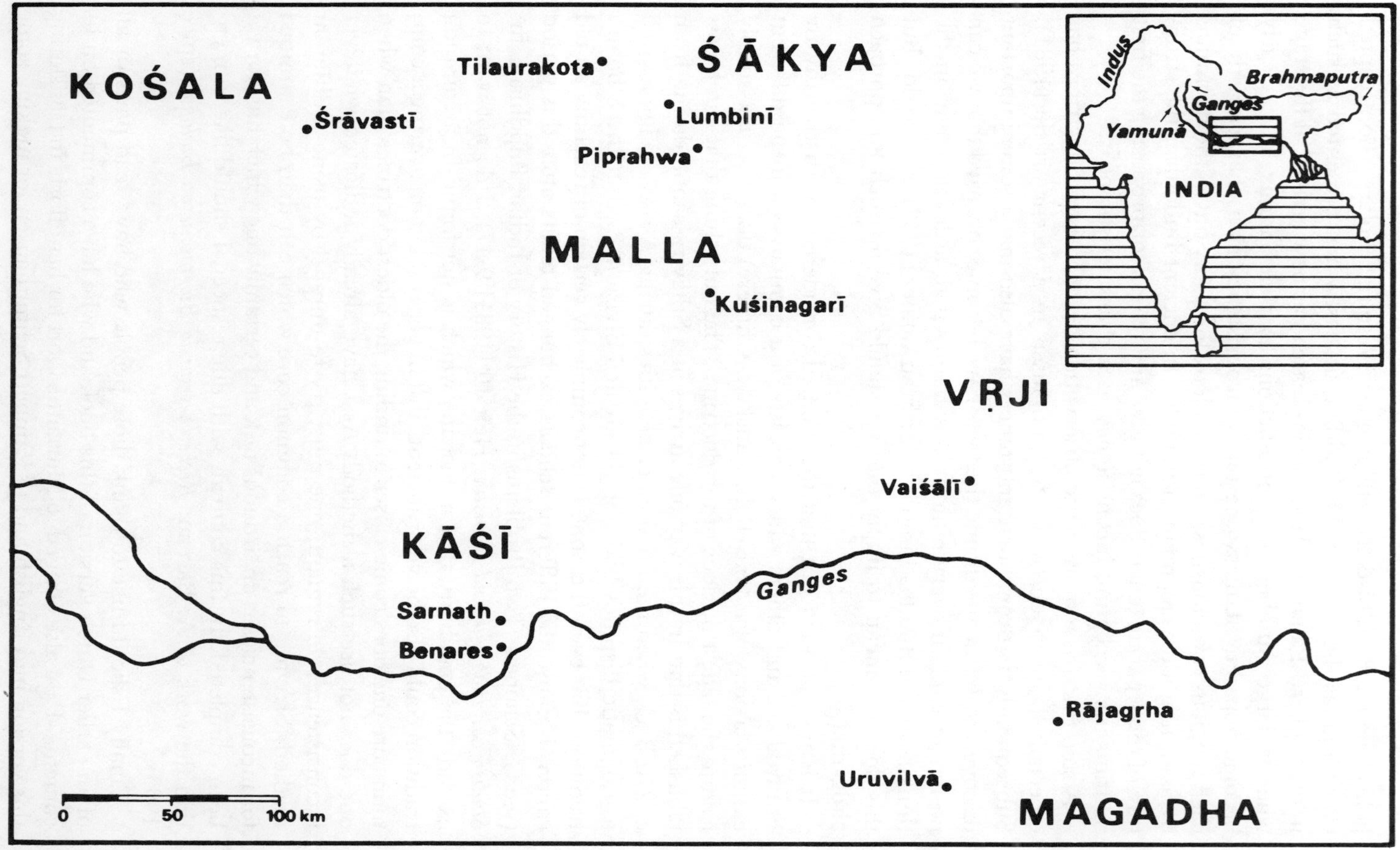
KOŚALA
Śrāvastī
Tilaurakota
ŚĀKYA
Lumbinī
Piprahwa
MALLA
Kuśinagarī
VṚJI
Vaiśālī
KĀŚĪ
Sarnath
Benares
Ganges
Rājagṛha
Uruvilvā
MAGADHA
0
50
100 km
Indus
Brahmaputra
Ganges
Yamunā
INDIA

# INTRODUCTION

I should like to give a brief survey of the following topics as background to the first chapters of this book: 1. biographical data on the Buddha, 2. the origin of the Buddha legend, 3. the expression "to seek salvation" which I use in describing the goal of the historical Buddha.

## *1. Biographical data on the Buddha*

Certain biographical information relating to the Buddha, including geographical names, can be accepted as being historically correct. But it is not easy to date things accurately from what is found in ancient texts. At present the following historical summary seems to be more or less acceptable[1]. The Buddha, mostly known by the name of Gotama, was born in Lumbinī[2] as the son of Śuddhodana, who was a prominent member of the Śākya (P. Sakya, Sakka, Sākiya) clan ruling in this area but probably under the dominion of Kośala. His youth was spent in Kapilavastu (P. Kapilavatthu)[3], where he later married and had a son named Rāhula. He left domestic life before his thirtieth year to become a wandering religious mendicant. For many years he sought to find a means by which salvation could be obtained and even practised extreme forms of castigation. He finally found a path to salvation. In the so-called Deer Park (the modern Sarnath) near Benares he acquired the first students of his teaching (*dharma*)[4] which was meant more as a guide to personal experience than a theoretical truth. In the course of the years he travelled through Kāśī, Kośala and Magadha and the territories of the Śākyas, Mallas and Vṛjis and established an order (*saṅgha*) of monks and later also nuns. At this point the names of the following disciples should be mentioned: Śāriputra (P. Sāriputta), Maudgalyāyana (P. Mogallāna), Ānanda and Devadatta. In all probability Śāriputra was

---

[1] Though not completely without reservations, for more details I recommend the chapter called "Date et vie du Buddha Śākyamuni" in E. Lamotte, Histoire, 12-25.

[2] With the exception of "Gotama" the Sanskrit (abbreviation: S.) version of names is given. If the Pali version shows a great deviation, it is included in parenthesis with the abbreviation "P.".

[3] It is uncertain whether the ruins near the present Tilaurakota in Nepal are identical with Kapilavastu or the ruins near Piprahwa in India.

[4] A meeting with the Ājīvika Upagu (P. Upaka) prior to this is found in the transmission. In agreement with Bareau (Recherches 1963, 155-160) one can accept that the Buddha did not say the beautiful verses attributed to him on this occassion, but he seems going too far by denying that the meeting ever took place. (See O. v. Hinüber, Die Erforschung der Gilgit-Handschriften, Göttingen 1979, 31-32).

largely responsible for developments connected with the method of discriminating insight (S. *prajñā*, P. *paññā*). Maudgalyāyana was thought to possess great magical power. Ānanda was the Buddha's constant companion throughout his final years. All pronouncements on the doctrine which were considered to be proclaimed by the Buddha were later presented as being reported by Ānanda. Devadatta is said to have wanted to take over the supervision of the order from the Buddha; he advocated stricter rules of asceticism. He is reported to have made attacks on the Buddha's life.

Influential laymen and laywomen gave aid to the order. Apparently at a very early stage the monks had access to parks where they could build huts against the monsoon rains; this was the beginning of the Buddhist monastery (*vihāra*). The Buddha often stayed in Śrāvastī (P. Sāvatthi), the capital of the kingdom of Kośala, in Rājagṛha (P. Rājagaha), the capital of the kingdom of Magadha, and in Vaiśālī, the capital of the Vṛji confederation. He died about eighty years of age near Kuśinagarī (P. Kusinārā).

Jina ("conqueror") Mahāvīra the founder of Jainism also preached in the same area. According to Buddhist tradition he lived at the same time as the Buddha, but this is questionable. Ancient Buddhism does have certain elements in common with Jainism, especially some rules of asceticism. These rules could go back to the Jina or his predecessors. But in ancient Buddhism they function differently from those of Jainism. What is paramount in Jainism is that one abstains from karma ("work") and expiates karma that has already been done by self-mortification, thereby liberating oneself completely from the burdening and obscuring material particles which penetrate the soul through work. In Jainism the soul is bond to a cycle of rebirth through karma and is robbed by karma of its innate qualities such as all-knowing and bliss. In ancient Buddhism when one refers to bad deeds, one follows the same lines as found in Jainism. What is bad is determined as transgression of the rules of asceticism, primarily the rule that no harm should be done to another's person or property. Avoiding bad deeds, though, has a more direct function in ancient Buddhism (see chapter 6).

No trace of any influence from the oldest Upanisads can be found in what I consider the most ancient layer of Buddhism[5]. But there is some

[5] The possibility of some influence of the teaching "When all desires (*kāma*) in the heart dissolve, then the mortal becomes immortal, here he reaches the Brahman", found as a quotation (*tad eṣa śloko bhavati*) in the Bṛhadāraṇyaka-Upaniṣad IV 4 7, can not be dismissed. But this could also be a reflection of Buddhist teaching and added later on (cf. Kaṭha-Upaniṣad VI 14).
Arguments for the first possibility can be found in N. Aramaki's contribution to the panel

evidence of such influence in the method of discriminating insight (see chapter 9) and the technique of meditation in spheres (see chapter 12).

The traditional account of how the Buddha obtained enlightenment near Uruvilvā (P. Uruvelā, the modern Bodh-Gayā) has not been included in the foregoing short biography of the Buddha. As A. Bareau[6] has shown this story is not found in the oldest sources, but can be explained by other reasons.

Nowadays one can read in even the most basic dictionaries that the Buddha lived in or around the period 560 to 480 B.C. The basis of the calculation of these dates can be found in the Ceylonese tradition which maintains that the Buddha died 218 years before the coronation of Asoka, which would mean that he obtained ''nirvana'' (*nirvāṇa*, P. *nibbāna*), i.e. died, in the year 544 B.C. At present Western scholars have corrected this date because the date of Asoka's coronation can now be calculated with more accuracy (268/7 B.C.). According to tradition the Buddha lived for eighty years (e.g. MN 12 I, p. 82), so that the period of his life can be calculated as being from 566 to 486 B.C. Eventhough the opinion amongst scholars was that these dates were based on shaky historical grounds, they still felt the need to state a date and, in principle, saw no objection to their choice.

In a recent article[7] H. Bechert argued that there are great objections to such an approach. For instance, in ancient lists of Buddhist ''patriarchs'' there are not enough persons found to easily bridge the 218 years between the Buddha's ''nirvana'' and Asoka's coranation. The old lists of elders should be accepted as being more reliable than later attempts at dating the Buddha's life. In view of this fact Bechert poses that a second tradition should again be considered. This tradition originates in India itself and not on Ceylon and maintains that the Buddha died 100 years before Asoka's coronation. A period of 100 years may be considered suspicious and consequently any thought of its being a valid possibility may be ignored. But a period of a 100 years fits Bechert's

---

''Earliest Buddhism'' of the VIIth World Sanskrit Conference (Leiden, August 1987). It is called : Some Precursors of the Subconscious Desire in the Attadaṇḍasutta.

[6] Le Buddha et Uruvilvā in: *Indianisme et Bouddhisme*, Mélanges offerts à Mgr. Etienne Lamotte, Louvain-la Neuve 1980, 1-18.

[7] The Date of the Buddha reconsidered, in: *Indologica Taurinensia*, vol. X (1982) 29-32. Also see H. Nakamura, *A History of Early Vedanta Philosophy*, Delhi 1983, 33 (note 23, referring to H. Ui) and R. Hikata, *Studies in Buddhism and Buddhist Culture*, Naritasan Shinshoji 1985, 1-20. Just published (a more sceptical account of the whole matter): H. Bechert, *Die Lebenszeit des Buddha—das älteste feststehende Datum der indischen Geschichte?,* Nachrichten. der Akad. der Wiss. in Göttingen I Philolog.-histor. Klasse, Jahrgang 1986, No. 4.

observations better, and it does not need to be taken too literally. He proposes that the Buddha could have reached "nirvana" between 85 to 105 years before Asoka's coronation. It remains to be seen how Bechert will expand the evidence for his position and how he will make it concur with other facts in Indian history.

*2. The origin of the Buddha legend*

A schism took place in the Buddhist order a few decades before the coronation of Asoka. Amongst other things attributed to one group, the Mahāsaṅghikas, is the belief that the life of the Buddha is eternal and that the efforts to become an Arhat do not lead to impressive results[8]. This seems to point to an attempt to reach salvation through the worship of the *Buddha* and not so much through following a path proclaimed or approved by him. This approach appears to be founded on a feeling of security that the Buddha gave to his followers during his life. The members of the other group, who were called Sthaviras (P. *thera*) probably had a right to consider themselves the true inheritors of the Buddha's *teaching*. They now tried to salvage the ideal of Arhatship by devising a more difficult path to that goal. While following such an arduous path it could be useful to think of the Buddha as the (no longer living) preacher of salvation and the greatest example of one who had reached the goal. In this context the Buddha is not a manifestation of a supernatural being. But the Sthaviras probably learnt from the Mahāsaṅghikas that the divinity of the Buddha was extremely important for propagandizing the doctrine. Perhaps because of this aspect, they tried to compensate for the gap by creating miracle stories, even though these stories were not consistent with the sober doctrines they professed. As E. Frauwallner (*The Earliest Vinaya and the Beginnings of Buddhist Literature*, Roma 1956) has observed, the author of the "Skandhaka" seemed to be very influential in utilizing such beliefs for the purpose of propaganda even though he drew from older sources. The first part of the Pāli Vinaya is an (adapted) version of the "Skandhaka", which originally also contained the nucleus of texts such as the Catuṣpariṣatsūtra and the Mahāparinirvāṇasūtra. The "Skandhaka" is based on ancient data, but often gives an interpretation and an extension of the story which can only be explained by the desire to compete with others for reasons of propaganda. What does seem to be a reliable report is that shortly before the Buddha's death an earthquake took place and it is possible that the Buddha explained this as an omen of his imminent

[8] See Bareau, Les sectes, 58, 64.

decease. According to the "Skandhaka" this earthquake was *caused* by the Buddha's decision to finally enter nirvana. The Buddha took this decision after Ānanda had failed to ask him to continue his life until the end of this world period (op.cit. p. 156). Afterwards every important event in the life of the Buddha is connected with an earthquake (cf. DN 16, II p.107). This is only an example of a process of adaptation. I shall scarcely refer to the Buddha legend in the following chapters. The first volume of *Buddhismus* by H. Beckh (Berlin 1916) is still a good introduction to the Buddha legend; see also Lamotte, *Histoire* p. 713-759. The earliest Chinese transmission of the Buddha legend can be found in E. Zürcher, Het Leven van de Boeddha, vertaald uit de vroegste Chinese overlevering, Amsterdam, 1978 (without the episode of the death of the Buddha). See also U. Schneider, Einführung in den Buddhismus, Darmstadt, 1980, pp 46-56 for a discussion on the origin of parts of the legend.

### *3. The expression "to seek salvation"*

I should like to make a few comments on the goal of ancient Buddhism. In the next chapters I shall sometimes state that the ascetic Gotama searched for "salvation" and found it as the Buddha and thereafter proclaimed it. This word "salvation" is in the first place a summery of all kinds of vague positive concepts which are found in the texts[9]. Secondly the word "salvation" is chosen to erect a barrier against giving the negative terms (i.e., directed towards the avoidance of something) an absolute meaning, because they are predominant in the texts and are not vague. By frequently mentioning a negative objective—avoidance of rebirth, avoidance of suffering and death, and the avoidance of a transitory existence—the impression could arise that non-existence is better than existence and that this is goal enough. I do not deny that in the course of history some Buddhists were content with such an aim. But the majority always found this an unacceptable interpretation of the generally professed objective that one must overcome suffering. It is an objective where, indeed, there is always the danger of such a purely negative inter-

---

[9] I am especially thinking here of MN 26 (I p.163,32; 165,15;166,35) *kiṁkusalagavesī anuttaraṁ santivarapadaṁ pariyesamāno* (searching for that which is beneficial, seeking the unsurpassable, best place of peace) and again MN 26 (passim), *anuttaraṁ yogakkhemaṁ nibbānaṁ pariyesati* (he seeks the unsurpassable safe place, the nirvana). *Anuppatta-sadattho* (one who has reached the right goal) is also a vague positive expression in the Arhatformula in MN 35 (I p. 235), see chapter 2, footnote 3. Furthermore, *sotthi* (welfare) is important in e.g. SN 2.12 or 2.17 or Sn 269; and *sukha* and *rati* (happiness), in contrast to other places, as used in Sn 439 and 956. The oldest term was perhaps *amata* (immortal, immortality), see chapter 2, but one could say here that it is a negative term (compare note 10 in the section "An Outline...").

pretation, while it has the advantage of avoiding inadequate and misleading concepts which seem to be connected with positive objectives.

A special problem arises in connection with the way to salvation via discriminating insight (see chapter 9), as soon as it is stated that the sum of all parts of a person is not the self, while one does not know of a self separate from these constituents. In chapter 11 I show that the consequence of this reasoning might be that one who is delivered after death no longer exists. This conclusion can hardly be avoided, but it is not acceptable, probably because of the feeling that the Buddha could not have meant this interpretation. So one chooses to reject all theories about this question. At a certain point in history it is explictly stated that the self does not exist outside the constituents. One would now expect that it can no longer be denied that the path to deliverance ends in nothingness. Oddly enough at the same time one strives to make nirvana, which is the "extinction" of a person on account of the cessation of the constituents (the person sometimes being compared to a fire and the constituents to the fuel), an independent entity. At least it now is described as something that cannot be considered non-existent. In the 16th chapter of Buddhaghosa's Visuddhimagga (p. 431-433) one finds a rejection of the opinion that nirvana does not exist (*n'atth'eva nibbānam*), as well as a rejection of the opinion that it can only be destruction (*khaya*). It is then stated that, in truth, nirvana is by its very nature not non-existent (*paramatthena sabhāvato nibbānaṁ nāvijjamānam*). Finally a passage from the canon (Udāna 8.3, Itivuttaka 2.16) is cited, "O monks, there exists the unborn, the unbecoming, the uncaused, the uncreated. If this did not exist, than there would be no escape for the born, the becoming, the caused, the created."

The Buddhist doctrine of salvation though also concerned with the spiritual well-being here and now, seems firmly bound to the concept that one must continuously be reborn and die. If there is no rebirth, then one needs no path to salvation, because an end to suffering comes at death. And one can willfully make an end to life if there is unbearable suffering. But even if a modern Buddhist can no longer literally believe in rebirth[10], he can apparently still be a follower of the Buddha in a significant way on the basis of the rejection of the purely negative interpretation of the goal. One could formulate the point of departure and the goal in this manner: to believe in a natural inheritance that is not suffering and to strive for an experience in which and after which the fear that suffering will be without end can no longer arise.

---

[10] See *Buddhismus der Gegenwart*, hrsg. H. Dumoulin, Freiburg i. B. (Herder) 1970, 70 (Buddhadāsa in Thailand) and 138 (some Japanese Buddhists).

# LITERATURE AND ABBREVIATIONS

*1. Primary sources and abbreviations*

This book is based on the results of research in which Pāli, Sanskrit (both hybrid and classical) and Chinese texts were compared. Terms and quotations from texts in parenthesis are mainly Pāli, but there is a preference for Sanskrit when using important terms which are not translated, e.g., *nirvāṇa* (usually written without diacritical marks) in lieu of *nibbāna*, *karma* not *kamma*, *dhyāna* instead of *jhāna*, etc. Exceptions are the names Gotama for Gautama and Asoka for Aśoka.

The Pāli canon which has been transmitted in Ceylon, Birma and Thailand consists of a collection (*piṭaka*) of (stories about) the rules of the order (*vinaya*), a collection of sermons [and dialogues] (*sutta*), and a collection of schematizing discourses (*abhidhamma*). The Vinaya Piṭaka is prominent because it contains a few ancient suttas and some details of the Buddha's biography. My description is mainly based on passages from the Sutta Piṭaka. The following texts of the Sutta Piṭaka are cited in the chapters of this book[1].

DN = Dīgha Nikāya
MN = Majjhima Nikāya
SN = Saṃyutta Nikāya
AN = Aṅguttara Nikāya
From the Khuddaka Nikāya:
- Dhammapada
- Udāna
- Itivuttaka
- Sn = Suttanipāta
- Theragāthā
- Jātaka
- Apadāna
- Buddhavaṃsa
- Cariyāpiṭaka

The texts of the Abhidamma Piṭaka will not be treated in any detail.

Although I have mostly worked with the Nālandā Devanāgarī Pāli Series (1958-1961) for practical reasons, I have also given the sutta numbers and, for the larger suttas, the page numbers of the editions of

---

[1] For more information consult K.R. Norman, *Pāli Literature*, Wiesbaden 1983 (A History of Indian Literature ed. by J. Gonda, vol. VII Fasc. 2).

the Pali Text Society (PTS) with the exception of the AN and the texts of the Khuddaka Nikāya.

The name Pāli, which came into use only in more recent centuries, refers to a branch of a rather old Buddhist literary language. Another branch is "Buddhist Hybrid Sanskrit". Pāli was brought to Ceylon in the third century B.C. It apparently soon disappeared in the mainland. Due to lessening contacts with India it did not undergo the influence of Sanskritization as long as Buddhist Hybrid Sanskrit[2]. It is possible that authentic quotations of the Buddha have been transmitted to us in Pāli. But one has to allow for a certain degree of adaptation or mutilation. As far as reliability is concerned the Sanskrit transmissions are only slightly inferior to Pāli texts. Unfortunately there is much less material available in Sanskrit and the texts have often been subjected to a longer period of compilation and interpolation than the canonical Pāli texts. A large part of Sanskrit and middle Indian texts has been conserved in a, often not too precise, Chinese translation. Such a translation sometimes reflects a more ancient stage of development of a text. The editions of canonical texts in Sanskrit are mentioned in the footnotes. Their titles generally include the names of the places in which they were found, i.e., Nepal, Turfan, Gilgit or Tibet.

There are also non-canonical Pāli and Sanskrit texts which are quoted several times in this book:

Milindapañha = The Milindapañho ... ed by V. Trenckner, London, 1880, repr. 1962;

Visuddhimagga = Visuddhimagga of Buddhaghosācariya ed. by H.C. Warren, revised by Dh. Kosambi, Cambridge, Mass. 1950;

Abhidharmakośa(bhāṣya) = Abhidharm-Koshabhāṣya of Vasubandhu ed. by P. Pradhan, Patna 1967 (Tibetan Sanskrit Works Ser.VIII).

## *2. Secondary literature and abbreviations*

It is not my intention to give a complete bibliography of the literature available either here or in the footnotes. The classics in this field such as H. Oldenberg's *Buddha* and L. de La Vallée Poussin's *Nirvāṇa* and almost all contemporary research is made available via the literature mentioned in the footnotes. Schmithausen, 1981, also refers to a great deal of literature which has been written in Japanese. Here I should only like to

[2] See O.v. Hinüber, Die älteste Literatursprache des Buddhismus, in : *Saeculum* 34, 1983, 1-9. Also see, *Die Sprache der ältesten buddhistischen Überlieferung* (Symposien zur Buddhismusforschung,II) ed. H. Bechert, Göttingen (Abh. d. Akad. d. Wiss.) 1980. Lamotte *Histoire* 607-657, gives a summery of the questions involved.

mention works which are often quoted and which have been abbreviated, but not always consistently.

(A.) Bareau, *Recherches* = Recherches sur la biographie du Buddha dans les Sūtrapiṭaka et les Vinayapiṭaka anciens: de la quête de l'Eveil á la conversion de Śāriputra et de Maudgalyāyana, Paris 1963, II. Les derniers mois, le Parinirvāṇa et les funérailles, tome I + II Paris, 1970 + 1971 (Publications de l'Ecole Française d'Extrême-Orient, vol. LIII, LXXVII).

(A.) Bareau, *Les sectes* = Les sectes bouddhiques du Petit Véhicule, Paris 1955 (Publ. de l'Ecole Française d'Extrême-Orient vol. XXXVIII)

(J.) Bronkhorst, (The) *Two Traditions* = The Two Traditions of Meditation in Ancient India, Stuttgart 1986.

(F.) Edgerton, BHSD = Buddhist Hybrid Sanskrit Grammar and Dictionary, vol. II: Dictionary, New Haven 1953, repr. Delhi-PatnaVaranasi 1970

Festschrift (for) Walpola Rahula = Buddhist Studies in honour of Walpola Rahula, ed. by Balasooriya i.a., London 1980

(E). Frauwallner 1953 = Geschichte der indischen Philosophie Band I Salzburg 1953

(E.) Lamotte, *Histoire* = Histoire du Bouddhisme Indien, Des origines à l'Ère Śaka, Louvain: Leuven 1958, repr. 1967

(L.) Schmithausen 1981 = On some Aspects of Descriptions or Theories of "Liberating Insight" in Early Buddhism, in: *Studien zum Jainismus und Buddhismus*, Gedenkschrift für Ludwig Alsdorf, hrsg. K. Bruhn und A. Wezler, Wiesbaden 1981, 199-250.

WZKS = Wiener Zeitschrift für die Kunde Südasiens.

ZDMG = Zeitschrift der Deutschen Morgenländischen Gesellschaft

ZMR = Zeitschrift für Missionswissenschaft und Religionswissenschaft.

## AN OUTLINE OF THE MOST ANCIENT FORM OF BUDDHISM

I have chosen the "Geschichte der indischen Philosophie"[1] by Erich Frauwallner as the starting-point for my discussion. In the chapter called "Der Buddha und der Jina" (pp. 147-272) a serious attempt is made to consider one, long recognized, inconsistency found within the most ancient doctrines of Buddhism and to explain it as a development of the Buddha's thought (p. 196-197, 213-214). The gist of the problem is that in the doctrine of the four noble truths, rebirth and suffering are derived from craving ("thirst", S. *tṛṣṇā*, P.*taṇhā*). However, according to the twelvefold chain of dependent origination, ignorance (S. *avidyā*, P. *avijjā*) is the root cause of rebirth and suffering; craving is only a secondary cause. Frauwallner came to the plausible conclusion that the twelvefold chain of dependent origination was discovered and revealed by the Buddha some time after the Buddha first discovered and taught the four noble truths. Unfortunately we just cannot stop thinking at this point in the reasoning. In the last few years a whole series of inconsistencies in the transmission of the Buddha's word have been uncovered. Especially André Bareau[2] and, to a greater degree, Lambert Schmithausen[3] have pointed to serious incompatibilities. Consequently we are no longer able to simply attribute all these differences to a development in the Buddha's own thought.

In order to avoid making things too complicated, I should like to restrict myself to giving an outline of only three of the most striking tenets analysed by Schmithausen. Firstly, one is freed from all cankers—and later released from rebirth and suffering—when one has progressed through four stages of dhyāna-meditation and, at the fourth stage, realized three kinds of knowledge, or at least one kind, namely the knowledge of the four noble truths. Secondly, one is freed from all cankers—and later released from rebirth and suffering—when one has progressed through four stages of dhyāna-meditation and subsequently gone to four stages of formless meditation and when one finally achieves the cessation of apperceptions and feelings (P. *saññā-vedayita-nirodha*). Thirdly, one is freed from all desire—and thereby later from rebirth and suffering—

---

[1] E. Frauwallner, *Geschichte der indischen Philosophie*, Band I, Salzburg 1953

[2] A. Bareau, *Recherches*, Paris 1963, 1970, 1971

[3] L. Schmithausen, "On some Aspects of Descriptions or Theories of "Liberating Insight" and "Enlightenment", *Studien zum Jainismus und Buddhismus, Gedenkschrift für L. Alsdorf*, Wiesbaden 1981

when, with discriminating insight (P. *paññā*) one segments oneself in five constituents and recognizes each as being transient and therefore suffering, i.e. unsatisfactory, and, consequently, as not worthy of being called self or mine.

We see here that we are dealing with the path to salvation and not a theoretical scheme as we saw in the problem of craving or ignorance mentioned before. In Buddhism the path to salvation has long been considered as being manifold. It is even considered one of the great achievements of the Buddha that he indicated different ways of obtaining salvation for different types of individuals. I do not want to imply that the recognition of the different paths to salvation does not reflect the Buddha's teaching or his tolerance towards the ideas of others. But from a historical point of view it is obvious that all the paths to salvation found in Buddhism are not equally of the same chronological age and that not all have been preached by the Buddha. Therefore one can justifiably ask: which one is the oldest of the three above-mentioned paths to salvation and are these paths originally preached by the Buddha himself?

I think that the second tenet can be dismissed as not having been taught by the Buddha, at least not in an early period of his long career as a teacher. Johannes Bronkhorst shows in his article "Dharma and Abhidharma"[4] that the four stages of formless meditation which follow the four stages of dhyāna-meditation in the second tenet—indicating an adaptation of dhyāna to this type of meditation—do not appear in the oldest Abhidharma lists. These lists are older than the Abhidharma Piṭaka of the various schools and they also appear in Sūtras. This indicates that they contain important evidence. Furthermore, Bareau has shown that the wellknown story in which the Buddha is said to have experienced stages of formless meditation under the guidance of Ārāḍa Kālāma and Udraka Rāmaputra before becoming enlightened has no basis in historical fact[5]. Without having undergone the stages of formless meditation the ultimate point of this path to salvation, i.e. the cessation of apperceptions and feelings, is not possible. Therefore, what is being described here does not seem to be an ancient *Buddhist* means of finding salvation. It is, however, possible that at some time the nucleus of this method was accepted by the Buddha as a means (see Appendix).

Two possibly very old paths to salvation remain for our consideration. If I should now just ask which of the two is the oldest path, it would be difficult to find the answer. Both paths contain elements which belong to a younger period and therefore even such a strong observation that only

[4] J. Bronkhorst, "Dharma and Abhidharma", *Bulletin of the School of Oriental and African Studies*, London, vol. 48, Part 2, 1985, 305-320.

[5] *Recherches* 1963, 13-27.

the first-mentioned path is used in accounts of the *Buddha's* release must be postponed. I shall now repeat the description of these two paths, adding a few explanations along the way.

The one path purports that one is freed from all cankers—and later released from rebirth and suffering—when one has progressed through the four stages of dhyāna-meditation and when, at the fourth stage, one realizes three kinds of knowledge[6], or at least one kind, i.e. the knowledge of the four noble truths. In this example the dhyāna-meditation is described as being founded on an ascetic conduct (P. *sīla*, S. *śīla*), which, it is true, is not self-mortification, but is nonetheless so rigorous that it does not allow one to defend one's life.

The other path states that one is freed from desire—and thereby from rebirth and future suffering—when, with discriminating insight, one perceives the five constituents of one's person as being transient, and therefore suffering (i.e. unsatisfactory), and that because of this they can neither be the self nor belong to the self. Here nothing is said of dhyāna or any other form of meditation. Ascetic conduct is also not mentioned. Monks and nuns are being addressed, so some degree of ascetic discipline is presupposed, even though this is not necessarily completely identical with the preparation for the practice of dhyāna.

In both of the paths mentioned above we come up against elements that make it difficult to define either with the appellations "earlier" or "later". Schmithausen[7] points out that the path utilizing discriminating insight usually contains a description of the result obtained, which is derived from the path of dhyāna-meditation plus realization of a higher knowledge. At the end we find the words, "in the released [person] is the knowledge: *it* is released (vimutt*am* iti). Rebirth is destroyed." The use of the neuter "vimutt*am*" (*it* is released) does not refer to something previously mentioned in the text. But these sentences are also found in the dhyāna path where "vimutt*am*" appears in a discussion of the "cit-t*am*" (the mind).

In this instance the path of discriminating insight would be later than the dhyāna path. However, the above description of the result obtained is not essential to the path of discriminating insight, because the result was already referred to in a previous section: "whoever discerns the constituents of his person in such a way (i.e. as transient, etc.) will get enough of them, and having gotten enough of them he is freed from desire and thereby released (*nibbindati, nibbindaṁ virajjati, virāgā vimuccati*)". A decision as to what is earlier or later is not yet possible.

---

[6] In Dīgha Nikāya 8 and 10 even eight kinds of knowledge are mentioned
[7] L. Schmithausen, 1981, 219

One can also discern a later element in the path of dhyāna plus realization of a higher knowledge. Three kinds of knowledge and, in some places, one kind should be realized at the fourth state of dhyāna. One would then be free of the three, later four, cankers (S. *āsrava*, P. *āsava*) which cause rebirth. The three kinds of knowledge are: 1. the knowledge of previous human existences, 2. the knowledge that all beings die and are reborn in either heaven or the underworld according to their past deeds, 3. the knowledge of the four noble truths. When only one kind is referred to, it is the knowledge of the four noble truths.

Are the places where only *one* kind of knowledge is mentioned a condensation, or are they more original than the places where *three* kinds are found? Schmithausen points out that in the canonical reports of the Buddha's enlightenment, which use the path of dhyāna plus realization of a higher knowledge, the first two kinds of higher knowledge have the verb in the present tense, while the rest of the report, including the kind of knowledge of the four noble truths, has the verb in the aorist[8]. Consequently, we can consider the first kinds of knowledge as later additions. We now only have to deal with one form of knowledge, i.e. that of the four noble truths.

Realizing these truths is said to remove the cankers, the āsravas, and thereby effect release. These āsravas are: [desire for] existence, [desire for] objects of pleasure, and ignorance. Later a fourth āsrava, opinions, was added. Ignorance, which, in explaining rebirth, seems to be a younger term than craving, or its synonym "desire", appears here as a cause of rebirth. The nucleus of the path of discriminating insight only recognizes a release from desire. In this respect it seems to be older than the conception of the removal of cankers by comprehending the four noble truths. Nevertheless this does not mean that a decision can now be made as to what is earlier or later. This is because the tenet of the three āsravas—the two types of desire, and ignorance—also does not fit in with

---

[8] F. Enomoto, "The Development of the Tisso-Vijjā Thought in the Early Buddhist Scriptures", *Bukkyo Kenkyu XII*, 1982, 63-81. Here the author tries to weaken this observation by pointing to Anguttara Nikāya 8.11 where, according to most manuscripts, the present tense is also found in the description of the four stages of dhyāna, which precedes the description of the three kinds of knowledge. This instance does not detract from the value of the evidence found in other suttas. Could a text in which the same tense is used everywhere have been copied in such a sloppy manner at numerous places that in all these places the present tense only appears in cases of the first two kinds of knowledge? Or what could have been the intention to present these two kinds of knowledge in a different manner from the rest of the text? Moreover this sutta corroborates Schmithausen's theory insofar as the third kind of knowledge is in the past tense and consequently clearly distinguished from the other two kinds of knowledge.

the realization of the four noble truths by which these cankers are destroyed and therefore does not belong to the dhyāna path that contains the four noble truths. According to the doctrine of the four noble truths only craving (desire, perhaps divided into two types) is a cause of suffering, but not ignorance. Therefore, what must have been meant in an earlier stage is that by realizing the four noble truths the cankers are destroyed. The fact that ignorance does appear among the cankers must be due to a later development in connection with the appearance of the twelvefold chain of dependent origination.

Though the path of dhyāna plus realization of a higher knowledge is now considerably reduced in content, we still do not have an equally plausible path to salvation as found in the path of discriminating insight. Only after having found such a path may we be justified in comparing it with the other in respect to priority and possibly employ the observation that it is this path (and not the other) which is often used to describe the Buddha's own release.

What is the problem of plausibility at this point of the argument? If one interprets the text literally, one must realize the four noble truths in the fourth stage of dhyāna. In order to understand the problem one must pay attention to the description of the dhyāna-meditation and its preparation.

The prerequisites for dhyāna are that one must be a monk, that one does not bring harm to any living being, that one does not take anything that is not offered, that one is chaste, does not lie, and that one also respects other ascetic prescriptions. According to the text one achieves a non-sensual form of happiness by thoroughly observing all these precepts. One must also guard against becoming enmeshed in impressions of the senses and (sensual) thoughts. This conduct also brings about a non-sensual form of happiness. At the same time one must try to do everything with complete mindfulness (P. *sati*). If someone who behaves in such a way, seeks out a lonely place and sits down quietly, he only needs to remove a few traces of interference before he almost effortlessly enters the first stage of dhyāna. This first stage is a state of joy and happiness, which arises from separation (i.e. the previously practiced renunciation of objects of pleasure as well as the solitariness of the place), accompanied by contemplation and reflection. In the course of time contemplation and reflection cease, giving way to inner calm and becoming one of heart. Joy and happiness remain, though they are no longer explained by separation, but as originating from concentration (*samādhi*). This is the second stage. Then the joy disappears, but happiness conceived as physical well-being remains. This happiness is joined by equanimity and awareness (*sati*). This is the third stage. Finally even the feeling of happiness disappears and equanimity and awareness reach a state of perfection[9]. This is the fourth stage.

The problem is that already at the second stage of dhyāna, contemplation and reflection—one could also say every form of discursive

---

[9] This is an attempt to interpret the Pāli compound *upekkhāsati-pārisuddhi*. It is analysed as *upekkhā-pārisuddhi* plus *sati-pārisuddhi*, because equanimity and awareness are mentioned side by side in the description of the third dhyāna and both seem now to reach a state of purity or perfection. In chapter 4 of the Visuddhimagga (p.136) this compound is explained as "purity of awareness born from equanimity", but this does by no means exclude the purity or perfection of equanimity in this state (compare the end of the same paragraph and the section on *upekkhābhāvanā* in chapter 9 of the Visuddhimagga). The compound *upekkhā-sati-saṁsuddha* in the Pārāyana (Sn 1107) must also be mentioned in this connection. Here an "emancipation by liberating insight" (*aññāvimokkha*) which is "purified by equanimity and awareness" destroys ignorance (*avijjā*). As I have argued here and in chapter 8 below, this seems to point to a later stage of the development of the dhyāna stream; therefore, it would not be necessary to take into account this compound when analysing *upekkhā-sati-pārisuddhi*. But even if it were necessary and the meaning now became: purification by equanimity and awareness (cf. the Sanskrit version quoted in the discussion below), it would be no problem for my interpretation. For it is difficult to conceive of such a purification by equanimity and awareness, if both qualities themselves have not reached some perfection.

Assuming that such a perfection characterizes the last stage of dhyāna-meditation I must strongly disapprove of some remarks on the nature of the stages of dhyāna by Konrad Meisig in his "Das Śrāmaṇyaphala-Sūtra" (Wiesbaden, 1987), which in respect to the aim of making accessible the Chinese versions of this Sūtra is a very useful book. Meisig says (p.65-66): "Sieht man von den Attributen ab, die die vier Stufen der "Meditation" negativ bestimmen, [...,] sieht man fernerhin ab von den mit den ersten drei Stufen verbundenen Glückszuständen, von denen die vierte Stufe schliesslich frei ist, die also auch nicht das Ziel der Ausübung von *dhyāna* sein können, und konzentriert man sich auf die Eigenschaften, die *dhyāna* positiv bestimmen, so findet man eine recht willkürlich zusammengestellte Reihe wohlbekannter Termini. Die erste, vorbereitende Stufe der "Meditation" ist positiv durch Überlegungen und Erwägungen (*vitarka vicāra*) gekennzeichnet. Geistige Zustände, die von Überlegungen und Erwägungen begleitet sind, mögen auch dem nicht Meditierenden widerfahren. Dies als Meditation zu bezeichnen, ist hier lediglich Sache der Definition. Die zweite Stufe beinhaltet inneren Frieden (*adhyātma saṃprasāda*) und "Zusammenschluß des Geistes" (*cetasa ekoṭībhāva*). Für "Zusammenschluß des Geistes" wird hier als Synoniem auch *samādhi* angegeben. Diese zweite Stufe ist also nichts anderes als eine wortreiche Umschreibung des letzten Gliedes, eben *samādhi*, des Achtfachen Pfades der Predigt von Benares. Die dritte Stufe der "Meditation" greift ebenfalls auf den Achtfachen Pfad zurück, sie ist nichts weiter als "Achtsamkeit" (*smṛti*), verbunden mit Gleichmut (*upekṣā*), Bestandteil der schon erwähnten vier *brahmavihāras*. Während aber "Achtsamkeit" im Achtfachen Pfad als vorbereitende Übung den *samādhi* einleitet und *samādhi* am Ende des Erlösungsweges steht, werden hier die Dinge gerade in ihr Gegenteil verkehrt: *samādhi* wird zur Voraussetzung für "Achtsamkeit". Die vierte Stufe bringt nichts Neues, in ihr ist das Denken durch die "Achtsamkeit" und durch den "Gleichmut" der dritten Stufe gereinigt (*upekṣāsmṛtipariśuddhacitta*)."

Meisig's argument depends on the presuppositions that negations have no meaning and that positive terms always must have precisely the same meaning; moreover, he does not carefully look at (the transmitted versions of) the passage on the four dhyānas (e.g. in the main versions, see also p.46 of his book, the second dhyāna is called "born from samādhi" [*samādhi-ja*] and not samādhi). I want to make some remarks on the second presupposition (also present in the opinion [p.65] that "der Begriff *dhyāna* Gemeingut in-

reasoning—have disappeared; one is in a state of inner calm and oneness of heart. And yet, at the fourth stage the four noble truths must be realized in a form described by the words "this is suffering, this is the origin of suffering, this is the cessation of suffering, this is the path to the cessation of suffering." That is not to say that this stage cannot be the origin of an intuition of a truth or that in it one cannot be aware of the words of a truth (they may be presented to the mind in the same way as objects, feelings, etc.). But it is difficult to imagine how in that state of pure equanimity and awareness one can follow a prescribed scheme. It apparently produces a high degree of non-identification with everything presented to the mind. Originally this may have been the only ground of an experience of release. Being based on an ascetic discipline guided by a concern for the well-being of all living beings, it need however not lead to indifference in everyday life. Moreover, penetrating abstract truths and penetrating them successively does not seem possible in a state of mind which is without contemplation and reflection. If the assertion were that in that state *entities* (and not truths) are to be clearly seen, it would be less unlikely.

---

discher Religionsgeschichte ...ist"). To me it seems entirely inadequate with regard to descriptions of spiritual processes. The term *samādhi*, e.g., has a broad spectrum of meanings beginning with concentration in everyday life and ending with meditative concentration without thinking (e.g. the basis of the second dhyāna) and even without consciousness (cf. the distinction between *saṃprajñāta* and *asaṃprajñāta samādhi* in Yogasūtrabhāṣya I 17-18). When somewhere the term samādhi appears, we cannot simply equate it with another samādhi, though there may be great affinity. Even if nearly the same state is meant, there can be a difference in intensity or perfection. On the other hand, the same phenomenon may be meant by different terms. I see no problem to equate, indeed, the second and also the third and the fourth dhyāna with the "right samādhi", although the second dhyāna is not identified with samādhi, but called "born from samādhi" (*samādhi-ja*). This samādhi seems to be the beginning of a process of perfection which reaches its highest degree in the fourth dhyāna which is characterized by the purity of equanimity and awareness. I see no other means to explain what is meant by the "right samādhi". I must also reject, that the description of the second dhyāna is only a verbose paraphrase of the last member of the eightfold path. On the contrary, it is one of the few places where we can get some information on the meaning of the abstract term "right samādhi". Furthermore, Meisig is convinced that the third dhyāna would rather be a step back, because its description mentions the term *smṛti* (P. *sati*), which we also find in the seventh member of the eightfold path. He evidently sees the eightfold path only as a kind of road where various stations are reached and abandoned and cannot imagine that each element helps in some way to constitute the next one and thereby could be intergrated in it and in this way undergo a process of perfection. I see no difficulty in the fact that a kind of samādhi, which itself is founded on efforts for mindfulness (*smṛti*), forms the base of a more spontaneous awareness (*smṛti*). This awareness and equanimity, when developed into a state of purity or perfection, (in another reading: the mind purified by them) constitute the fourth and highest point of dhyāna and, very likely, of the "right samādhi" which also may be considered having stages.

Incidentally, this state of pure equanimity and awareness may also have been the origin of the method of discriminating insight. This method tried, however, to obtain non-identification through reasoning and not through dhyāna and later was at the most only assisted by some kind of dhyāna (see below). It is true, that this reasoning must be more than superficial theoretical reasoning and be accompanied by concentration, but it is not identical with the concentration called "right samādhi" which evidently goes beyond reasoning.

In order to solve the problem under discussion we should now make use of the observation that the Buddha's release is not at each place accounted for by means of the detailed description of the dhyāna path concluding with at least one kind of knowledge. There is one simple description where only the right samādhi is mentioned (without a subsequent perception of a describable knowledge). It is the noble eightfold path found in the beginning of the "first sermon" at Benares. It can be used, if we assume that the instructions to others found there originated from the Buddha's own experience and that he taught a method he himself had employed just before. This sermon, called "the setting in motion the wheel of the teaching" (P. *dhamma-cakka-ppavattana*), is a combination of instructions to others and an account of his full enlightenment. It is documented by a wide range of text traditions with variations, of which some will be discussed. However, the content of this sermon is such that one can hardly assume that this is precisely the way the Buddha's first teaching took place. The text progresses from a very simple description of practice (the middle way) to a kind of system of practice (the noble eightfold path, consisting of abstract terms which need some explanation), moving on to a theoretical framework of the system of practice (the four noble truths) and finally arriving at a definition of the Buddha's enlightenment (and, in some versions, also of his release, suggesting that the Buddha found salvation by the discovery of the four noble truths). Very likely the first section reflects the oldest teaching and the following sections subsequent stages.

The content of the first section of the sermon is as follows. In the deer park at Benares the Buddha meets five ascetics who had accompanied him earlier when he still practised self-mortification and who had expected him to find salvation through this method. When one day the Buddha gave up self-mortification, they interpreted this as renewed indulgence in sensual pleasure and turned away from him. The Buddha now wanted to prove to the ascetics that there was a middle way between self-mortification and sensual pleasure and that along this path "immortality" (as the goal is described here and not yet as the "cessation of suffering''[10]) is found. Other reports in ancient scriptures, as well as the next section of this sermon, show that this middle way not only implied avoiding extremes (nowhere do we find that the Buddha was interested in moderation as such), but also the possibility of perceiving something in the middle that one normally does not observe, i.e. very likely the potential, inherent in everyone, of practising dhyāna-meditation. According to Majjhima-nikāya 36, the Buddha, when he no longer saw any sense in self-mortification, remembered experiencing *non-sensual* happiness in his youth and this led him to a possible path to salvation. He did not abandon the concept that sensual pleasure is not beneficial. But when a convincing path to salvation presented itself, he no longer thought it necessary to avoid non-sensual happiness. In order to follow this path that, as far as he knew, no one had followed before, he had to take a step that was inconceivable to his former companions: he began to eat sufficient food again. Along this path he progressed through different stages of non-sensual happiness and finally reached a state of complete equanimity and awareness and (very likely) the experience of having found salvation. The section under discussion shows that he wanted to share this experience (which in MN 36 seems to be indicated by the term *bodha*) with his former companions. Majjhima-nikāya 26 reports the same attempt. This text contains the short address on immortality which is also found in Vinaya I p.9, but then only tells us that the Buddha is so busy instructing the five ascetics that he no longer goes out begging himself, but continually two or three of the five ascetics must bring back food for the others. The text does not mention what he is teaching, but I cannot imagine the Buddha constantly repeating the short lessons that have come down to us in the ''first sermon'' at Benares or other dogmatical constructs. This report only becomes meaningful to me if I assume that he was initiating these ascetics in the stages of dhyāna-meditation and was guiding them in a very practical way.

---

[10] Compare Shozen Kumoi: Der Nirvāṇa-Begriff in den Kanonischen Texten des Früh-Buddhismus. *WZKSO* XII-XIII (1968-69, 205-213.
As K.R. Norman observed in his contribution to the panel Earliest Buddhism of the VIIth World Sanskrit Conference (Leiden 1987) the translation ''immortality'' (for *amata/amṛta*) perhaps gives a wrong impression. This may especially be true with persons who only know the immortality of Greek gods. But looking at the usage of *amata* in ancient India and supposing that it was also the usage of the Buddha's environment which he had, to some degree, to take into account, I feel obliged to reproduce the ambiguity of *amata*. Though the denotation of *amata*, viewed from the development of dogmatics, can only be ''never dying again after this death'', it is not very likely that the audience felt only this when hearing the word. And the Buddha must have known that it did not only convey the etymological sense of ''un-dying''. He probably did not intend that people hoped for individual immortality, but also did not want to convey the idea of total annihilation, when using this word.

Let us see if the next section of the "first sermon" can contribute to our search. Here the middle way between sensual pleasure and self-mortification is explained as to its contents. It is said to be the noble eightfold path, i.e. right views, right resolve, right speech, right conduct, right livelihood, right effort, right mindfulness, and right samādhi (concentration). Here we deal with a more complicated state of the preaching. However, if we look at the last, and in my opinion the most important, component of this list, we are still dealing with what according to me is the real content of the middle way, dhyāna-meditation, at least the stages two to four, which are said to be free of contemplation and reflection. Everything preceeding the eighth part, i.e. right samādhi, apparently has the function of preparing for the right samādhi. It appears to have become necessary to explicitly deal with this preparation. We can assume that in the case of the Buddha the conditions were such, that he was able to call up dhyāna and progress forward in it only on the basis of the intuition of the possibility of a middle way between sensual pleasure and self-mortification. In the beginning he also tried to teach in that way. But soon he gained disciples who after the teaching of the middle way, were not able to achieve a state of dhyāna and could not be led to further stages. He now had to think about his own conditions, which were not yet fully conceptualized.

The scheme of the noble eightfold path can be understood as the result of this attempt. On the basis of *the right views* about afterlife and a possible path to salvation one must take the *right resolve* to leave the housely state. But even then one could not just simply go somewhere and sit down and call up a state of dhyāna. According to a comparable portion of the detailed description of the dhyāna path a state of non-sensual happiness which is the starting-point of dhyāna-meditation is only available through unconditionally fulfilling the disciplines of asceticism,such as not doing harm to any being, etc. Even before the time of the Buddha some ascetics had followed these same precepts, but apparently only with the purpose of avoiding bad karma and mixed with selfmortification, so one can hardly speak of achieving a feeling of happiness. The Buddha's method is practised without self-mortification. *Right speech, right conduct and right livelihood* lead to non-sensual happiness. Moreover, *right effort and right mindfulness* are also helpful in reaching the right samādhi.

Now comes the next step in the teaching. The noble eightfold path achieves the right samādhi and thereby obviously a feeling of being freed from rebirth and redeath. But is there also a logical ground for this feeling? It is. To show this seems to be the main reason for the establishment of the theoretical framework of the four noble truths which proclaim a first cause of suffering, the possibility of the destruction of this cause (and thereby of suffering) and the noble eightfold path as the way to bring about this destruction. Another motive could have been to be more explicit with respect to the starting-point of all striving for release; it was evidently more than only "mortality" which could be derived from the word immortality first used to state the goal. But if this framework was mainly induced by the question about the logical ground for feeling released in and after the right samādhi, this would point to growing concern about the invisible goal of release from rebirth after death. This concern is not altogether absent in the first section of the "first sermon", but there, at the end of the short address on immortality, the experience of having reached the aim of *brahmacarya* here and now (*diṭṭhe va dhamme*) seems to dominate. Even the term *amata/amṛta* (immortality), though very likely denoting absence of future dying, is of such a nature, that one text (Lalitavistara p. 409) can combine it with the word *sākṣātkṛta* ("directly perceived"; compare *amatam adhigatam* in the Pāli version). Most interested in this question were in all probability persons who had not (yet) reached the right samādhi. Persons who have obtained the fourth dhyāna which is characterized by pure equanimity and awareness are not likely to worry much about the destruction of the first cause of rebirth, though they will accept it as a welcome completion of their experience of a state without fear for the future. But this theory was not only important for beginners of the dhyāna path, it was also valuable for adepts of the path of discriminating insight, provided this method was already practised at that time. One can imagine this when, in an early state, it had only the aim of non-identification. However, the earliest forms of discriminating insight transmitted to us were established only after the introduction of the four noble truths, because their explicit aim is overcoming rebirth by conquering desire.

The noble eightfold path now becomes provided with a theoretical framework in the form of the four noble truths. It is the last of these truths. The first three truths indicate: a) the condition at the onset, b) the first cause of this condition, c) the aim of avoiding this condition by destroying the first cause. The fourth truth is the means to destroy the first cause.

a) The starting-point is a series of natural events which are designated by the word suffering and which can hardly be avoided. These are birth, growing old, illness, death, etc. b) But these events are not *completely* inevitable. They occur because at some point one did desire continuation of pleasure in a new existence. The cause of a new existence is this desire or craving, and consequently this is also the cause of all events which are irredeemably connected with existence. c) The goal is the cessation of these events by ending this craving which leads to a new existence.

The person, who reaches the right samādhi at will and with ease, now also theoretically knows that rebirth is destroyed. The restlessness within his heart, the craving for pleasure and existence, has been overcome and this craving is now known as the cause of rebirth. This situation is best reflected by a formula found in MN 26 (see also below): "Imperturbable (P. *akuppa*) is my heart's release (P.*me cetovimutti*), this is my last existence, now there is no longer rebirth".

The four noble truths seem to have originated mainly from the necessity to remove theoretical doubts. But they are not pure theory. At least not, if we take seriously what is said in the fifth section of the "first sermon". If we do so and accept it as being, in the nucleus, the words of the Buddha, we learn how he himself thought about the way these truths originated. For him they were what in modern times we would call intuition. Besides such an expression as "the [inner] eye arose" (P. *cakkhuṃ udapādi*) the term "unsurpassable, complete enlightenment" is found in this section. This term seems to contain a revision of the term enlightenment as it is used in the earlier sections of the "first sermon". The Buddha says: "It was not until I saw each of the four noble truths in these three ways [see below] that I maintained that I had reached the unsurpassable, complete enlightenment". This is an interpretation of the fifth section that seems to make more sense than the traditional view that he found release by discovering the four noble truths. This view does not agree with the demand, contained in this same discovery of the four noble truths, that one must cultivate the noble eightfold path. It is based on the last part of the fifth section (not found in all versions), where the Buddha's imperturbable release is called a result of this discovery, which could be accepted insofar as, even for the Buddha himself, the last theoretical doubts had to be removed. However the opinion that he obtained his first and authentic experience of release by discovering the four noble truths seems wholly due to external influence (see below).

The content of the fifth section is: the Buddha discovered the four noble truths previously revealed to no one—suffering, the origin of suffering, the cessation of suffering and the path to the cessation of suffering. Moreover, he saw what had to be done with each truth—one must fully understand suffering, one must abandon the origin of suffering, one must realize the cessation of suffering and one must practise the path to the cessation of suffering. Finally, he saw that he had done all this—he had fully understood the truth of suffering, he had abandoned the origin of suffering, he had realized the cessation of suffering, and he had practised the path to the cessation of suffering. Only after he had observed all this did he claim to have reached the unsurpassable, complete enlightenment and [not in all versions:] knew: the release of my heart is imperturbable, this is my last existence, there is no longer rebirth.

In the Mūlasarvāstivāda-vinaya this section appears before the section where the four noble truths are taught and explained. This gives a logical impression, but it is not likely that this is the historical sequence. The account of the Buddha's full enlightenment is best understood as a reflection on the discovery of the four noble truths and the implications of this discovery and as an adjustment of the term enlightenment (it now is called unsurpassable) to this discovery. Before this discovery the term *buddha* (with various prefixes) meant that a path to "immortality", the middle way, was found and, shortly after, "immortality" realized (see chapter 5; cf. Lalitavistara p.409: *amṛtaṃ mayā bhikṣavaḥ sākṣātkṛto*[sic] *'mṛtagāmī ca mārgaḥ, buddho 'ham asmi*). Thus it was established that this path was the right one. Enlightenment and experience of release were closely connected here. The unsurpassable enlightenment of the fifth section does however, if the above interpretation is correct, not effect, but at the most affect, an experience of release; it only removes theoretical doubts. This is not the interpretation adhered to by those followers of the dhyāna path who gave, after some time, the detailed description of this path its final shape. In their understanding the Buddha was not released until he had discovered the four noble truths. The same persons perhaps added to the account of the Buddha's full enlightenment the formula about the imperturbability of his release, which is not found in all versions.

But why this traditional interpretation? Very likely the cause was the growing influence of a non-Buddhist spiritual environment which claimed that one can be released only by some truth or higher knowledge. In addition, the alternative (and perhaps sometimes competing) method of discriminating insight (fully established after the introduction of the four noble truths) seemed to conform so well to this claim.

I have discussed a particular problem of one transmitted path to salvation, i.e. how one can perceive the four noble truths at the fourth stage of dhyāna. Insofar as an older stage of the same path to salvation ends in the right samādhi, this is only a fictitious problem. The fact that it came to such a problematic formulation is probably due to the influence of an environment that demanded some truth or knowledge as the real means of release.

Must one then consider the path of dhyāna plus realization of a higher knowledge as merely the product of a literary tradition? It could have functioned as a practical means to salvation if one first had used the four noble truths as a guideline for meditation and had strived thereafter to rise above discursive thinking. But this situation is not very likely. Such an interpretation becomes still more unlikely at the next stage in the development of this path to salvation, where the realization of the other kinds of knowledge is added, the knowledge of one's past human existences and of the disappearance and rebirth of other creatures in heaven or in the underworld according to their deeds. The disagreement of these two kinds of knowledge (see chapter 14) and the above mentioned philological argument, that these two kinds of knowledge are described in a different tense from the rest of the detailed description indicates that in this stage we are dealing with a predominantly literary product. Nevertheless the structure of dhyāna plus realization of knowledge subsequently was given a function in the praxis, i.e. in the path of discriminating insight (which however is not realized in, but immediately after a higher state of dhyāna, see below). Before I can discuss this further, I must turn back to the oldest form of discriminating insight (S.*prajñā*, P.*paññā*) which has nothing to do with this structure.

The same section of the Vinaya, in which the sermon of "the setting in motion of the wheel of the teaching" appears, continues with a second sermon at Benares, the topic of which is the path of discriminating insight, but without any allusions to dhyāna or samādhi. From the context we can derive that this sermon does not contain the oldest of the Buddha's tenets. In this Vinaya text we find a tradition of discriminating insight that does not know how to deal with the contents of the different sections of the "first sermon", but does not dare to put this "first sermon" on a secondary level or put it aside completely. Just what is the case? Here we find that the "first sermon" is not understood as an encouragement to practise dhyāna or the eightfold path culminating in the right samādhi—the way I understood the text on the basis of the words in this sermon—but it has the exclusive purpose of making the audience aware of the transientness of all things (as if even one word was said on this subject) and, in doing so, inducing them to become a member of the Buddhist order (this is also unknown to the text of the "first sermon"). The first listeners find salvation only after hearing the contents of the "second sermon", dealing with discriminating insight, and even without having to perform anything at all, but only through listening and understanding; understanding while listening or immediately thereafter effects salvation once and for all.

The path of discriminating insight developed through various stages. Two such stages are apparent in the "second sermon" at Benares. First we find that the constituents of a person may not be called "self" (or, must be called "non-self"), because they bring along suffering and because one does not have power over them. Then it is stated that one must not consider the constituents as belonging to the self or as the self, because they are transient and therefore suffering, i.e. unsatisfactory. The first argument found little response, but the second argument later became the essence of the Buddha's message for many Buddhists.

The introduction of the path of discriminating insight probably is connected with difficulties involved in practising the real dhyāna and its preparations. Instead of this a simpler method was devised (very likely by the Buddha himself) and offered to most of the disciples, namely the method of judging the constituents of the person as non-self. Moreover, this method was said to release one from desire (and therefore from rebirth) as soon as one has fully understood the fact that the constituents are not the self.

However, this simple method was not without a price. It is not surprising that in this context one did no longer speak of the imperturbable (P. *akuppa*, S. *akopya*) release of the heart and that later on doubts arose whether just having discriminating insight once was enough to do away with desire and other cankers, eventhough desire and other cankers are at that moment and shortly thereafter no longer present. The release of the heart (P. *cetovimutti*), being concerned with life here and now, is explained here by "release through discriminating insight" (P. *paññāvimutti*), and one can justifiably ask what value it has in moments of serious threat or pain. Even leaving such moments aside, the conduct of persons, who considered themselves to have found salvation because they had followed that method, was not always irreproachable. Out of these problems arises the next development as one attempts to find methods by which the path of discriminating insight gains more depth. The Abhisamaya-vāda of the Sarvāstivādins is an example of such an attempt (see E. Frauwallner, Abhidharma-Studien III, *WZKS* XV, 1971). The "perfection of discriminating insight" (S. *prajñā-pāramitā*) in which the transientness of all things is radicalized to the unreality of all things could also have had originally this aim.

A third method, perhaps the oldest in this development, was to use dhyāna-meditation, which is based on ascetic conduct (P. *sīla*), in aid of the path of discriminating insight (P. *paññā*). The scheme *sīla-samādhi-paññā* has especially become well-known through the structure of the famous Visuddhimagga (c. 400 A.D.). It is already found in a few passages in the canon (e.g. DN 10). In the Visuddhimagga it is meant as a succession of practices: first ascetic conduct, then meditation (mainly by concentrating on a special object), and finally[11] discriminating insight.

[11] The Visuddhimagga makes a distinction between the state of meditation as such, where discriminating insight is not possible, and a concentrated mind immediately after such a state; cf. p.311: ...*samāpattito vuṭṭhāya samāhitena cittena vipassissāmā ti*... See also

We may assume that in ancient times it functioned in the same way.

There are, however, some suttas (e.g. MN 64) which teach that discriminating insight is realized in (not: after) a higher stage of meditation. The realization of discriminating insight here appears to have the same position as the realization of the four noble truths in some other suttas. The problems mentioned above with regard to the latter are still greater here. Discriminating insight is much more in need of some kind of reasoning than realizing the four noble truths. One has to learn that whatever is transient is unsatisfactory, and whatever is unsatisfactory is non-self. Such reasoning seems impossible in higher stages of dhyāna. Therefore I cannot help considering these suttas purely literary products (see chapter 12).

Where dhyāna was really practised in aid of discriminating insight, it seems to have been practised as a preparation for this insight. That dhyāna is followed by discriminating insight implies that this dhyāna no longer comes into being in the old way, because after the highest stage of dhyāna in the old sense there is no need for discriminating insight. It is not denied that ascetic conduct is a prerequisite also to this new dhyāna. But it is a prerequisite in order to guarantee the quietude necessary before one can enter a more artificially produced dhyāna. In the Theravāda tradition one is directing oneself especially to the practice of "kasina" exercises, i.e. one concentrates on pure elements and colours. These exercises were the first steps of the (above-mentioned) path which via four stages of dhyāna and four stages of formless meditation culminates in the cessation of apperceptions and feelings. That implies that one reaches a kind of dhyāna which can be characterized by pure form (*rūpa*), and which can be transformed into meditations without any form. But pure form is not mentioned in the description of the stages of dhyāna in the dhyāna path.

Persons who practised discriminating insight preceded by dhyāna tried to refer to the noble eightfold path for this practise. Sometimes it was interpreted as containing *paññā*. *Paññā* can, however, only be inserted into the first two members of the eightfold path. Because for these persons the path to salvation culminates in discriminating insight and not in the right samādhi, they must conclude, as did the nun Dhammadinnā in MN 44

---

p.890 note 43 in Nyanatiloka's translation of the Visuddhimagga (Konstanz 1952) commenting on *appanāyaṁ ṭhatvā vipassanaṁ vaḍḍhento* (Visuddhimagga p.153): "D.h.nachdem er aus der vollen Sammlung wieder herausgetreten ist, denn während der Vertiefung erlangt man keinen Hellblick (*vipassanā*) in die Vergänglichkeit, das Elend und die Unpersönlichkeit der 5 Daseinsgruppen." Compare Schmithausen, 1981, 242.

(contrary to, e.g., DN II p.216-217), that the eightfold path is no path which one has to traverse from one stage to the next, but only a list of important means.[12]

---

[12] In the canon (e.g. many suttas in AN 10) we also find passages where the eightfold path is enlarged by two more members, knowledge (*ñāṇa* which may be the realization of the four noble truths or discriminating insight) and liberation (*vimutti*).

# I. DHYĀNA-MEDITATION

CHAPTER ONE

# THE BUDDHA FINDS THE MIDDLE WAY, I.E. THE DHYĀNA-MEDITATION

One of the most trustworthy passages[1] of the Buddha's biography as it has been handed down to us describes how the ascetic Gotama realizes after years of increasingly more stringent forms of self-chastisement that this is a fruitless attempt to find salvation and at that moment remembers an experience from his youth (MN 36, I p. 246):

> "Then, Aggivessana, I thought: I remember that once when my father, the Sakka, was working (in the fields), I was sitting in the cool shadow of a Jambu tree. Separated from objects which awaken desire, separated from harmful qualities[2] I reached a (state of) joy and happiness (*pīti-sukha*) accompanied by contemplation and reflection which is the first dhyāna (meditation)[3] and remained in it for some time. Could this be, perhaps, the way (*magga*) to enlightenment(*bodha*)? After this memory, Aggivessana, I had this knowledge: this is the way to enlightenment. [Then], Aggivessana, I thought: why should I be afraid of this happiness that has nothing to do with objects which awaken desire and nothing to do with harmful qualities. [Then], Aggivessana, I thought: I am not afraid of this happiness that has nothing to do with objects which awaken desire and nothing to do with harmful qualities."

The memory of an experience in his youth is described in the stereotype terms which became common usage in Buddhism for the first stage of dhyāna. It is not very probable that the Buddha experienced this at that time in the exact form as described or that he thought of it as the first step of a series towards some goal. But there appears to be little doubt as to the nucleus of this story. It is the memory of a state of joy and happiness while he was quietly sitting somewhere; the remembrance of a state which was due to the absence of disturbing objects as well as disturbing emotions. The environment was such that one could tranquilly observe a thing and contemplate it.

---

[1] Compare P. Horsch, Buddhas erste Meditation, *Asiatische Studien* 17, 1964, 100-154; A. Bareau, *Recherches* 1963, 47-48; J. Bronkhorst, *The Two Traditions*, 16.

[2] *Akusalā dhammā* probably means desire, hate, etc. Compare the description of the control of the senses in the elaborated path to salvation, e.g. MN I p. 180, 29: *abhijjhādomanassā pāpakā dhammā*.

[3] P. *jhāna*. For another (Jain?) use of the word, which never applies when I refer to *dhyāna/jhāna* see the polemic passage in MN 36 I p. 243,4: *yan-nūnâhaṁ appānakaṁ jhānaṁ jhāyeyyan-ti* etc., . J. Bronkhorst in *The Two Traditions* (Chapter: The ascetic practices of the Bodhisattva) discusses the question at some length.

At some time or other many of us will have experienced such a state; a few moments of happiness without desire while looking at the landscape or a work of art. The slightest attempt to perpetuate this state by trying to possess the object observed puts an end to it. Such a state does not go together with egotistical desires and cares. But through years of practising self-mortification, Gotama, the ascetic, had reached a state of mind which enabled him to turn this memory into a new experience and to intensify and transform it.

According to the account in MN 36 there were still two obstacles that had to be removed before achieving this new experience, an ascetic prejudice and his poor physical condition.

The ascetic prejudice was that one could reach salvation only through pain (whether by patiently suffering it or through selfmortification) and not by happiness[4]. Gotama, too, was of the opinion that one could not achieve salvation through worldly happiness because it is dependent on "objects of desire" (*kāma*). For this reason he left his home and became a wandering religious mendicant and would always remain one.

But for years he had tried in vain to reach salvation through pain. He went to the extremes of self-mortification[5] and after some time became convinced that he would not find it by such methods. It appears that he was searching for a soteriological experience that is a release in the present life as well as regarding an after-life and he could not accept a dogma which stated that by suffering pain now he would be released at some time or other. But the memory from his youth offered a third possibility besides worldly happiness and self-mortification. It was a state of bliss that was not dependent on the objects of desire; that was even only possible through the absence of any desire. That is why, in the passage quoted above, the question is asked, "Why should I be afraid of this happiness...?" and the answer is, "I am not afraid of this happiness...".

The second obstacle was his poor physical condition which was caused by long periods of fasting. As the text states further on, he thought that this happiness could not be reached and retained if one had a weak body. For this reason he again started to eat healthy food. His change of attitude towards eating caused five ascetics, who until now had followed him with great respect and had expected him to reach salvation, to leave him.

---

[4] Compare MN 14 (I p.93): *Na kho āvuso Gotama sukhena sukhaṁ adhigantabbaṁ, dukkhena kho sukhaṁ adhigantabbaṁ.*

[5] At least for the possiblities known to him. It is not necessary to believe everything written in the texts about the Buddha's selfmortification in order to show that also objectively he had done his utmost.

After he had strengthened himself with food, he evoked the state he had remembered from his youth. According to later terminology he had reached the first stage of dhyāna-meditation at that point.

After some time the contemplation and reflection characteristic of the first stage ceased. Internal calm (*ajjhattaṁ sampasādanaṁ*) and oneness of the heart (*cetaso ekodibhāvo*) had taken over. A feeling of joy and happiness still remained but it was now evidently resulting from concentration (*samādhi*), whereas, in the first stage, it was attributed to separation without any internal or external disturbance. This was called the second stage of dhyāna.

Afterwards the interest for the feeling of joy (*pīti*) disappeared and with it the feeling itself; he became equanimous (*upekhaka*), aware [of everything going on] (*sata*) and acutely perceptive (*sampajāna*). But he still experienced happiness (*sukha*) through his body (*kāyena*). This was called the third stage of dhyāna.

Finally he gave up physical happiness and achieved the state of perfect equanimity and awareness (*upekkhā-sati-pārisuddhi*) which was experienced as being as far removed from happiness and cheerfulness as from pain and depression. This became known as the fourth stage of dhyāna.

In this way he intensified and transformed a state which seems to be, in principle, accessible to everyone. Pure equanimity and awareness were the only remnants of a happiness which had arisen from separation. This was something he felt to be the first to discover. But did he also find what he had been seeking all these years, the highest salvation, the deliverance from rebirth? According to most texts which mention this event he had not yet completely found it. According to these sources he had to use his transformed state of mind to reach a liberating insight which could be expressed in words. Most texts say that he now discovered the four noble truths or three kinds of knowledge of which the knowledge of the four noble truths is the highest.

These different kinds of knowledge will be treated in later chapters (8 and 14). The four noble truths may have their origin in this state of mind. However, they do not teach that one is released by knowing the four noble thruths, but by practicing the fourth noble truth, the eightfold path, which culminates in the right samādhi. As we shall see, this right samādhi was interpreted in various ways. But a later branch of thought, which relied on a dogmatic approach rather than on the psychological description referred to here and which did not want the proclaimed truths to be seen as products of reflection, denied any freedom of interpretation. It tried to place words and concepts directly in the liberating experience of the Buddha. In the next chapter we shall see that probably the word "immortality" (*a-mata*) was used by the Buddha for the first interpretation of this experience and not the term cessation of suffering that belongs to the four noble truths.

An assertion in SN 2.12 also points to a liberating experience which in the beginning was not formulated in words: those who possess the dhyāna [meditation] (*jhāyino*) shall no longer be subject to death (*maccu*).

A very ancient assertion seems to be that even one who is in the first stage of dhyāna can no longer be seen by Māra (MN 25), or has freed himself of Māra's power (AN 9.4.8.). Here, also, no dogmas are discernible. Māra is probably a very old, Buddhist personification of death (at any rate, it cannot be accounted for in Hindu mythology or by the development of Buddhist dogmatics). The two places mentioned make almost the same statements as SN 2.12.

This also points to the fact that the Buddha did not achieve the experience of salvation by discerning the four noble truths and/ or other data. But his experience must have been of such a nature that it could bear the interpretation "achieving immortality" or (later) "cessation of suffering" used for his own orientation and for proclaiming this goal to others.

CHAPTER TWO

# THE FIRST SERMON

In the previous chapter I showed some hesitation in following the traditional view that the liberating experience of the Buddha had been expressed in words. The structure of the "first sermon" also supports this reluctance.

In the sermon named "putting in motion the wheel of the teaching" (*dhamma-cakka-ppavattana*), which has been documented in a broad spectrum of texts, we can, if we include the introductory story, discern five parts which show a remarkable sequence[1]. The doctrine of the four noble truths is the fourth part, whereas the fifth part contains a report of how the Buddha found these truths and became fully enlightened (and, in some versions, was liberated).

One can distinguish the following parts in the sermon:

1. Gotama finds the five ascetics that abandoned him when he broke his fast
2. The middle way
3. The noble eightfold path
4. The four noble truths
5. The Buddha's full enlightenment

"The middle way" (part 2)—interpreted by me as dhyāna-meditation (see below)—appears to be the nucleus of the Buddha's teaching. It is placed in an increasingly larger frame in parts 3 and 4. Part 5 defines full enlightenment as the discovery of the four noble truths (part 4) and speaks of the fulfilment of all implications of this discovery. Parts 3 to 5

---

[1] Mahāvagga of the Pāli Vinaya, I p. 8 ff.(the starting-point of my analysis)
SN 56.11 (without part 1) = Vinaya I p. 10 ff.
Mahāvastu ed by Senart, tome 3, Paris 1897, p. 328 ff.
Lalitavistara ed. by Lefmann, Halle 1902, p. 407 ff. (excerpts from the Mahāvastu and Lalitavistara are included in F. Edgerton's Buddhist Sanskrit Reader, New Haven 1953, p. 17 ff.; he, too, pointed out the compilatory character of the Dhamma-cakkappavattanasutta)
Probably the oldest Chinese version is Taisho 196 (Vol IV), 148a14-149a12, see E. Zürcher, Het Leven van de Boeddha, Amsterdam, 1978, p. 113 ff.(a very corrupt version)
Saṅghabhedavastu in the Vinaya of the Mūlasarvāstivādins, ed. by Gnoli, Roma 1977, I p. 133 ff. (here we find part 4 after part 5 and included in the second sermon; the same sequence and details are found in the Catuṣpariṣatsūtra, ed. by Waldschmidt, Berlin 1962, "Vorgänge" 11-14, see R. Kloppenborg, The Sūtra of the Foundation of the Buddhist Order, Leiden 1973 p. IX-XIII and 21-29).
Compare Bareau, *Recherches* 1963, 161-189.

will be treated in the following chapters. I will now first discuss part 1 and then part 2; one can find the report of part 1 also in MN 26 (I p. 171-173).

The beginning of the Dhamma-cakka-ppavattana-sutta gives the impression of being historically acceptable. It can be found in all versions. The Buddha introduces himself as Tathāgata to his former companions and proclaims to have found immortality. The short address on immortality cannot be found in the Vinaya of the Mūlasarvāstivādins (and related texts). It has instead, after the rejection of speaking to a Tathāgata as "friend" and by name, a threat with calamities, if someone does so. But note that even in this Vinaya, in verses preceding that chapter, the theme of immortality can be found (Saṅghabhedavastu ed. Gnoli p.129: *apāvṛṇīṣva amṛtasya dvāraṃ*, p. 130: *apāvariṣye amṛtasya dvāraṃ*, cf. Vinaya I p.5-7 and MN 26, I p.168-169), which, though situated in a mythological context, could be a reminiscence of the first teaching. The Vinayas of the Mahīśāsakas and Dharmaguptakas (see Bareau, Recherches 1963, 163-164) and the Lalitavistara have both the threat and the address on immortality.

The Buddha arrives in the deerpark close to Benares. From a distance the five ascetics see him arrive and decide that they will not rise up and greet him in respect. They remember that he had broken his fast, which to them was a sign that he had returned to worldly abundance. But as the Buddha comes closer, they cannot contain themselves. They rise and greet him with the words "Be welcome, friend Gotama". At this the Buddha says, "Do not speak to the Tathāgata[2] by name or as "friend". The Tathāgata is an Arhat[3] and completely enlightened. Listen! Immor-

[2] *Tathāgata*, literally "thus-gone" (tathā-gata) [later also interpreted as "thus-come" (tathā-āgata)], originally seems to have been a term for someone who no longer would be reborn. This is clearly seen in MN 22 I p. 140, 3-6 (see end of chapter 9), as well as in MN 72 where the question "does a Tathāgata exist after death? does he not exist?" is examined and, in I p. 468,21, *vimuttacitto ... bhikkhu* is found instead of *tathāgata*. It is probably the first term the Buddha employed to designate himself, as one can derive from comparing all versions of this section. Very soon it became a title which was reserved for the Buddha (later, the Buddhas). In the first meeting with the five ascetics the Buddha very likely used this term with the intention: I am a "thus-gone", i.e. am a person who had such an experience, as you yourselves always expected me to obtain; I now deserve all respect and cannot be spoken to as "friend" or by name. However it is probable that in the Pāli version some editing has already occurred. Following this version I feel obliged to speak of *the* Tathāgata and to translate: *the* tathāgata is ( = I am) an Arhat ( = released). If the Buddha was the first person to use this designation, its occurrence in Jainist suttas could be explained with the aspect of having gone the way to salvation. In Buddhism however the aspect of solely having found the way to salvation became dominant.

[3] After Tathāgata had become the title for the Buddha, Arhat (S., P. araha), literally "one who is worthy" became the term to designate someone who will no longer be reborn.

Later this word acquires the following predicates (e.g. MN 35 I p. 235, 10): he has over-

tality is found (*amatam adhigatam*); I proclaim, I teach the Dharma[4]. If you do what I proclaim, already in this life (*diṭṭhe va dhamme*) you will soon know, realize, and remain in possession of the highest goal of the holy life (*brahmacariya*) for which noble men[5] leave their homes." Furthermore the Buddha explains to the five ascetics that breaking his fast was not a return to worldly abundance and finally brings them to the point when they will listen to what he has to say.

In MN 26 it is not related what he taught now. It is only stated that two or three of the five ascetics would at times get food for all and that the Buddha continuously taught those present. The Dhamma-cakka-ppavattana-sutta can be of help to us on this point. There the middle way (the second of the aforementioned five parts of the sutta) follows the words of the Buddha just related above.

First the two extremes are described which must be avoided by all who have abandoned their homes (*pabbajita*). One must not surrender oneself to the pleasures of the objects of desire, which is low, vulgar, ordinary, ignoble, and harmful. Nor should one surrender oneself to the mortification of one's own body, which is painful and (though not low, vulgar and ordinary) is (still) ignoble and harmful. By avoiding these two extremes the Tathāgata discovered (*abhisambuddha*) the middle way, which opens one's eyes, makes known, and leads to tranquility, to insight, to enlightenment (*sambodha*), and to Nirvana[6]. What is this middle way?

---

come the cankers, he has reached perfection (in religious life), he has done what should have been done, he has cast off the burden, he has reached salvation, he has destroyed all fetters tying him to existence, he is released through right insight (*khīṇāsavo vusitavā katakaraṇīyo ohitabhāro anuppattasadattho parikkhīṇabhavasaṁyojano samma-d-aññāvimutto*).

[4] In many passages *dharma* (S., P. *dhamma*) can be translated as teaching or doctrine in the sense of a rule of conduct to be practised (less in the sense of a theoretical truth). A few lines further we find the word *dhamma* used in the meaning "state", *diṭṭhe va dhamme*—literally, already in this seen state—means already in this life. In the plural *dhamma* sometimes means "pyschic qualities" (as we have seen in the previous chapter) and "things" in general; in most schools of Buddhism the basic entities, the elements or factors of existence are called *dhamma/ dharma* (pl.).

[5] *Kulaputta* (P., S. *kulaputra*), literally son (P. *putta*) of ( = belonging to) a (good) family (*kula*). This word and its feminine form *kuladhītā* was probably used in the same sense as "noble" (*ariya*) that originally meant someone of the higher social classes, but in Buddhism was employed for persons of high moral standards without taking social class into consideration. Giving a moral or spiritual meaning to current terms was probably a trait of the Buddha's style of preaching. But because this trait can easily be imitated one can only cautiously use it as a criterion of authenticity.

[6] Not all of these (quasi-)synonyms necessarily date from the most ancient period; the oldest forms probably are at the beginning of such series of terms (see chapter 4 on nirvana). Note, however, that there are also attempts to understand such series as states in a spiritual development. In his contribution to the panel "Earliest Buddhism" of the VIIth World Sanskrit Conference (Leiden, August 1987) K. R. Norman interpreted the series *nāyaṁ dhammo nibbidāya na virāgāya na nirodhāya na upasamāya na abhiññāya na sambodhāya na nibbānāya saṁvattati* (MN 26 I p.165) in such a way.

Here, the text passes to the next part distinguished by me where it is stated, "It is the noble eightfold path." This is a series of eight concepts, culminating in "right samādhi", which will be treated in the next chapter.

For the time being we have a simpler answer to the question of what is the middle way. Very probably in the beginning only the "right samādhi", a term which I consider nearly synonymous to dhyāna-meditation[7], was mentioned and not the diverse means to reach that end. I assume that in his first sermon the Buddha started out from the premise that stating the extremes which must be avoided would more or less automatically lead to the third possibility of something midway, the dhyāna-meditation. A further task was to intensify and transform the first stage of dhyāna-meditation which had been revealed by hinting at the middle way. He had to describe further stages and to guide his diciples. That he no longer begged for food himself, as mentioned in MN 26, and continuously taught two or three of the five ascetics, does not point, in my opinion, to a dogmatic form of instruction, nor to a continuous repetition of the description of the stages of dhyāna, but to an intense guiding of the process of meditation within the framework of these descriptions[8].

---

[7] Compare note 9 in An Outline of the Most Ancient Form of Buddhism (above).

[8] On this point my interpretation completely deviates from the end of the Dhamma-cakka-ppavattana-sutta which is presented as a whole. According to the Pāli Vinaya version the only thing which the Buddha achieves with the "first sermon" is that one of his audience, Koṇḍañña becomes possessed of a pure "Dharma eye" in that "all that is subject to origination, is subject to destruction"; this results in Koṇḍañña wanting to become the first member of the Buddhistic congregation. The continuous teaching which we also find in this text results in the other four members of the audience—first two and then again two—becoming possessed of the Dharma eye as well and also wishing to become members of the order. Here release from the cankers and thereby from rebirth takes place only after listening to and understanding the "second sermon" (Vinaya I p. 14, "*imasmiṁ ca pana veyyākaraṇasmiṁ bhaññamāne pañcavaggiyānaṁ bhikkhūnaṁ anupādāya āsavehi cittāni vimucciṁsu;* cf. chapter 9 on discriminating insight). In other words it does not take place by meditation nor after listening to a sermon that encourages one to practise meditation. But encouraging meditation with all the passages added to it is transmitted as the *first* sermon in this tradition which is connected with discriminating insight and which hardly knows what to do with it. As to this first sermon, one can therefore be certain that one is dealing with a more ancient doctrine.

In the Vinaya of the Mūlasarvāstivādins (Saṅghabhedavastu ed. Gnoli I p. 137-139) the proclamation of the four noble truths has the result that one of the audience, Ājñāta-Kauṇḍinya, was released from all cankers (and thereby from rebirth) by listening to this proclamation (not by practicing the eightfold path culminating in "the right samādhi" belonging to these truths). The rest of the five ascetics was released by listening to the sermon about discriminating insight.

CHAPTER THREE

# THE NOBLE EIGHTFOLD PATH

So far two of the five parts of the Dhamma-cakka-ppavattanasutta have been considered, finding the five ascetics again and the first sermon in the form of proclaiming the middle way.

We now come to the third part, the noble eightfold path. This path consists of a series of eight concepts:

1. right views (*sammā-diṭṭhi*)
2. right resolve (*sammā-saṅkappo*)
3. right speech (*sammā-vācā*)
4. right conduct (*sammā-kammanto*)
5. right livelihood (*sammā-ājīvo*)
6. right effort (*sammā-vāyāmo*)
7. right mindfulness (*sammā-sati*)
8. right samādhi(concentration) (*sammā-samādhi*)

Obviously this series contains all kinds of directions for reaching point (8), right samādhi. The difference between the middle way and the noble eightfold path can possibly be explained in the following way. The Buddha will have observed that merely communicating the insight which led to his discovery was not enough for everyone. Consequently he had to search for ways to reach a (joyful) state of mind which could serve as the starting point for the dhyāna-meditation. The points he thought were important were apparently gathered together in the noble eightfold path[1]. But this does not mean that he would have preached in such a manner. These are only subjects for instruction and, as such, mean little or nothing.

Because the text of the Dhamma-cakka-ppavattana-sutta does not enter upon this point, it seems permissible to look for an explanation at other places in the canon. I will not choose passages which explain the eight concepts in the style of commentaries, as such devices point to later developments and, moreover, often contain little concrete information[2]. It seems to me that the best way to handle the examination is to place a detailed description of the dhyāna path to salvation[3] which appears in

[1] Compare AN 7.5.2. where the first seven points are interpreted as an aid to "the right samādhi"; the same idea is found in DN 18 (II p.216) and in MN 117 (III p.71).

[2] E.g. MN 141 or DN 22 (II p. 312) or MN 117.

[3] See chapter 6 note 1.

several passages in the canon alongside the noble eightfold path and to see which elements agree or show a similarity. This detailed description has itself undergone serveral stages. Even certain elements which can be compared with ideas in the noble eightfold path can have details which were added later. For this reason some degree of caution is desirable and I shall restrict myself to a short explanation. The reason why I choose to interpret these passages in a particular way will become clear later in chapter 6 in which a corresponding passage of this detailed description of the path to salvation will be under consideration. The fact that the nucleus of this passage coincides with the noble eightfold path is, on the other hand, a reason for me to consider it the oldest stage of the detailed description of the dhyāna path.

Under these conditions an interpretation of the noble eightfold path may be given as follows:

1. right views: the belief that not all comes to an end with death[4] and that the Buddha proclaimed a path to salvation which he, himself, had successfully followed,
2. right resolve: leaving home and trying to follow this path as a religious mendicant,
3. right speech: not lying, not using rude language, not telling the one person what another has said about him and thereby possibly alienating the two persons, only speaking about things that are necessary and which can serve salvation,
4. right conduct: not killing or injuring, not taking what is not given, not performing sexual acts.
5. right livelihood: living from begging, but not accepting everything and not possessing more than is strictly necessary.
6. right effort: guarding against the possibility that sensual impressions or sensual thoughts should receive any attention.

---

[4] Compare AN 10.17.10 (Nal. ed. IV p. 320,26): "He has the right views (*sammādiṭṭhiko hoti*), he does not see things in a wrong way: that which is given exists, that which is sacrificed exists, that which in poured (into the fire) exists, the fruit, i.e. retribution for good and evil actions, exists, the world, here, exists, the other world exists, the mother exists, the father exists, beings who appear (spontaneously) exist, in the world ascetics and brahmans exist who have gone and followed the right path and who describe this world and the other world from their own experience and realization."

This formula contains rather archaic formulations (cf. chapter 14). It is an inversion of the teaching of Ajita Kesakambala (cf. DN 2, I p.55). In MN 117, III p.72, one can see how it is supplanted by a new definition of right views. It points especially to the consequences of our actions in the "other world". But the final sentence makes it possible to introduce the idea that one can trust in the Buddha as one who, through his own experience, has found a path out of this world *and* the other world (the beginning of the elaborated path to salvation, see chapter 6).

7. right mindfulness: being completely conscious of everything one does, not being absent-minded.
8. right samādhi: the four stages of dhyāna meditation as described before (to put it more accurately, the first dhyāna seems to provide, after some time, a state of strong concentration, from which the other stages come forth; the second stage is called *samādhi-ja*).

Probably one does not have to follow the directions strictly in sequence, some things can be done simultaneously. But it is difficult to prove that there was no sequence at all and, therefore, no path. Later, when the means "discriminating insight" (P. *paññā*, S. *prajñā*) was introduced and partisans of this method tried to find this means in the noble eightfold path, they did have to interpret this series as purely a collection of concepts. "Discriminating insight" is not included in the series. If one, nevertheless, feels obliged to find it there, one can only interpret the first two concepts in such a way. The nun Dhammadinnā did this already in MN 44 (I p. 301). A tradition of reinterpreting the noble eightfold path in this sense commences from this point and continues on till modern times. In his "Buddhistisches Wörterbuch" (Konstanz, 1953) the venerable Nyanatiloka translates the first two concepts as "rechte Erkenntnis" and "rechte Gesinnung" which makes it possible for him to find the means "discriminating insight" in the noble eightfold path. As he considers "discriminating insight" to be a higher means than "the right samādhi", there remains little choice but to give up the idea of a path that must be followed step by step (op. cit. p. 120-121)[5].

---

[5] Buddhists who are susceptible to textual argumentation are referred to AN 10.11.3 (and 10.12.9) where a path is explicitely taught, because after right views, follows right resolve; after right resolve, follows right speech, etc. Actually I do not consider this a very original sutta and will not include it in my argumentation.

CHAPTER FOUR

# THE FOUR NOBLE TRUTHS

The four noble truths[1] are a theoretical frame in which the noble eightfold path (and consequently also the dhyāna-meditation) has been set. They resemble (but need not historically depend on) the kind of theoretical frame a doctor could use to explain his therapy. The starting point is (1) a certain kind of disease. One looks for the cause of the illness (2). Then one attempts to cure the disease by removing the cause (3). In order to achieve this one uses a particular therapy (4).

Analogous to this the Buddha now states the four noble truths; this is the fourth step in the Dhamma-cakka-ppavattana-sutta. The four noble truths are:

1. suffering (*dukkha*)
2. the origin of suffering (*dukkhasamudaya*)
3. the cessation of suffering (*dukkhanirodha*)
4. the way leading to the cessation of suffering (*dukkhanirodhagāminī paṭipadā*).

The Dhamma-cakka-ppavattana-sutta itself gives a few explications as to the meaning of these four truths.

The noble truth of suffering is explained as: "Being born is suffering, becoming old is suffering, being ill is suffering, dying is suffering, being joined to unpleasant [persons and things] is suffering, being separated from pleasant [persons and things] is suffering, not getting what one wishes is suffering"[2].

The noble truth of the origin [ = the cause] of suffering is explained as: "It is this craving (*taṇhā*, S. *tṛṣṇā*)[3] which leads to rebirth, which is connected with pleasure and desire, which finds pleasure here and there"[4].

---

[1] The problems in regard to the precise wording were recently discussed by K. R. Norman: "The Four Noble Truths: A Problem of Pāli syntax", *Indological and Buddhist Studies (Festschrift de Jong),* Canberra 1982, 377-391.

[2] At the end of this explanation we find, "in summery, the five constituents, to which one clings, are suffering". But this does not wholly match with the preceding enumeration of things which are actually painful, and may be considered a later interpolation from another interpretation of suffering ( = unsatisfactory). See chapter 9 on discriminating insight.

[3] The word taṇhā can also sometimes be translated as "appetite for", e.g. in DN III p. 85 (see D. Franke, Dīghanikāya, Göttingen 1913, 277).

[4] Only in the Pāli version this is followed by, "namely the craving for objects of desire (*kāma-taṇhā*), the craving for existence (*bhava-taṇhā*) and the craving for non-existence (*vibhava-taṇhā*)."

The noble truth of the cessation of suffering is explained as: "It is the cessation of this craving through complete detachment, the abandoning (of this craving), the rejecting, the breaking loose from, the not holding on to (this craving)".

The noble truth of the way (*paṭipadā*) which leads to the cessation of suffering is explained as "It is the noble eightfold path (*magga*)". Then the concepts "right views", etc., follow as mentioned in the previous chapter.

Note the fact that the way (*paṭipadā*) to the cessation of suffering is explained by the eightfold path (*magga*) and that this means to overcome suffering is mentioned at the last place and not the result.

It is also remarkable that (at the third place) the result is described in such a brief and exclusively negative manner. The word *amata* (immortal, immortality) that probably was used in the beginning (see chapter 2), perhaps suggested, at least left some possibility for a positive representation of the state of being saved. This is no longer true for the expression "cessation of suffering through the cessation of craving", which could point to an increased interest in the invisible result of never being born again.

Sometimes the concept S. *nirvāṇa* / P. *nibbāna* (being extinguished, being put out) is used to explain the third noble truth. It appears as the sixth of six synonyms in the second part of the first sermon (see above) and was possibly added later to this series. When it was first used, it seems to have been more a figure of speech than a concept; a definition of the term is scarcely to be found. As a figure of speech it conveys the meaning that as craving or a wrong attitude ceases, it is like a fire which has been extinguished. Sn 1109 could be considered one of the first applications to the third noble truth. A statement made by Śāriputra (SN

---

When the craving is specified in the Pāli canon, it usually appears in these three forms (e.g. MN I p.49.1; 299,20; III p. 250,34; DN II p. 61 and 308; SN III p. 26).
The first two types of craving correspond to *kāmāsava* and *bhavāsava* in the series of the three cankers (see chapter 8) and to *kāmarāga* and *bhavarāga* in the series of the seven proclivities (*anusaya*) in DN III p. 254. But something corresponding to the third type, craving for non-existence, is not to be found in this kind of series. The possible origin of this division is discussed in T. Vetter, "Some Remarks on older parts of the Suttanipāta" (forthcoming). See the Appendix of this book.
The Sarvāstivādins, at least the later ones, also know the term *vibhava-tṛṣṇā*: Abhidharmakośa(bhāṣya) V, 11a; the commentary explains it as "craving for transience (*anityatā*) which seems to correspond to "craving for non-existence".
In the Pramāṇasiddhi chapter (verse 184) of the Pramāṇavārttika Dharmakīrti refers to an ancient division of craving, *bhava-*, *kāma-*, *vibhava-icchā*.
In Indonesia the concept *vibhava-tṛṣṇā* appears once in an inscription; see Prasasta Indonesia II, Selected Inscriptions from the 7th to the 9th Century A.S. by J. G. de Casparis, Bandung 1956, 111 and 133 (*vibhava* is translated as "power"; compare A. L. Basham, The Wonder that was India, London 1954, reprint 1961, 269).

38.1) is often quoted where he says that nirvana is the destruction of desire, hate, and confusion. A second meaning of nirvana is the ceasing of rebirth, e.g., in Sn 1094 , "the destruction of aging and death I call nirvana". The first meaning of nirvana does not always contain a purely negative idea. This can be seen in two verses of the Suttanipāta (1086-87),

> "O Hemaka, if you completely repulse the desire which strives for pleasant things ..., then this is the everlasting abode of extinction (*nibbānapadam accutaṁ*).
> Those who, as mindful [persons], have realized this are already here and now extinguished (*diṭṭhadhammābhinibbuta*) and at rest for all time; they have overcome attachment to the world."

Probably only after the introduction of the analysis of the person into five constituents (see chapter 9), one distinguished between these two meanings in the following way: the first was a nirvana with a remainder consisting of possessions (P. *upādi*, S. *upadhi*) [i.e. constituents and other things] and the second was a nirvana without this remainder.[5]

[5] An attempt is made to summarize all this in the prose passages of the Nibbānadhātusutta of the Itivuttaka (2.17). There are two kinds of nirvana, *sa-upādisesa* and *nir-upādisesa*. *Sa-upādisesa* is described with the Arhat formula mentioned in chapter 2, note 3; here one still perceives as others, but no longer is subject to desire, hate, and confusion. The Arhat formula also holds for *nir-upādisesa*, but there, in addition, all feelings disappear. Note that in the introductory prose of the Dvayatānupassanāsutta of the Suttanipāta we find the sentence, *diṭṭheva dhamme aññā, sati vā upādisese anāgāmitā*. Here, *upādi* has the (perhaps older) meaning "possessiveness"; a remainder of this *upādi* prevents a person from entering nirvana immediately after death.

CHAPTER FIVE

# THE BUDDHA'S FULL ENLIGHTENMENT

The fifth and last section distinguished by me in the Dhammacakkappavattana-sutta is a record of the Buddha's full enlightenment (and, not in all versions, of his release). The beginning of this section in the Pāli Vinaya (and also in the Vinayas of the Mahīśāsakas and of the Dharmaguptakas, see Bareau *Recherches* 1963, 174-177) can be summarized as follows:

Thus the Buddha relates, I discovered suffering, this, up to now, unknown noble truth; I discovered that this noble truth must be fully understood; and I discovered that this noble truth has been fully understood. I discovered the origin of suffering, this, up to now, unknown noble truth; I discovered that this noble truth is to be abandoned; and I discovered that this noble truth has been abandoned. I discovered the cessation of suffering, this, up to now, unknown noble truth; I discovered that this noble truth is to be realized; and I discovered that this noble truth has been realized. I discovered the path to the cessation of suffering, this, up to now, unknown noble truth; I discovered that this noble truth is to be practised; and I discovered that this noble truth has been practised.

In the Mahāvastu, the Lalitavistara and the Saṅghabhedavastu ( = SBV) the same matter is arranged otherwise: Thus the Buddha relates, I discovered the, up to now, unknown [four noble truths (only SBV)], suffering, the origin of suffering, the cessation of suffering, and the path to the cessation of suffering. I discovered, moreover, that [I(only SBV)] must fully understand suffering, must abandon the origin of suffering, must realize the cessation of suffering and must practise the path to the cessation of suffering. Finally I discovered that [I] had fully understood [the noble truth of] suffering, had abandoned the origin of suffering, had realized the cessation of suffering, and had practised the path.

The end of this section in the Pāli Vinaya can be summarized as follows: It was not until I saw each of the four noble truths in these three ways that I maintained that I had reached the unsurpassable, complete enlightenment (*anuttaraṁ sammāsambodhiṁ abhisambuddho*) and knew: imperturbable is my heart's release (*akuppā me cetovimutti*), this is my last existence (*ayam antimā jāti*), now there is no longer rebirth (*natthi dāni punabbhavo*). All the other versions mention the unsurpassable, complete enlightenment (or an equivalent), but the Vinayas of the Mahīśāsakas and of the Dharmaguptakas say nothing about release. Mahāvastu, Lalitavistara and SBV speak about release, but SBV does not call it imperturbable.

The authenticity of the last part of this section, "imperturbable is...", is subject to doubt, when one compares the various transmissions. Moreover, it is not very likely that the Buddha had not already obtained the result mentioned in this part[1]. Supposing that he felt himself released after having reached a state of pure equanimity and awareness, we cannot assume that he only felt himself released after having discovered the four noble truths in such a way. But one must not exclude the possibility that the original text contained an allusion to a (more theoretical) certainty of being released. The rest of the report (perhaps originally less schematized) together with such an allusion (or without it) could make sense in the following way.

The Buddha told his audience that, in retrospect, he could not be considered fully enlightened and released beyond any (theoretical) doubt as long as he had not discovered the scheme of the four noble truths, had not recognized the practical implications and made sure that in his own case (which is the standard for others) all was already done that was implied. That is to say that he revised an earlier concept of enlightenment after having discovered the four noble truths. It is possible that he, after a first experience of release and after having developed a path to help others, felt some need to assure himself and others as to the invisible effect that can be reached by this path. Only after he had found the four noble truths, he may have become fully convinced (and told his disciples so) that he had discovered all that was necessary. Why? The four noble truths contain a new element, the belief that craving was the cause of rebirth, besides arranging what was known and practised until now. Therefore, feeling himself released after having reached a certain state of mind he now also knew the reason, why he felt so: in this state he had overcome craving.

As to the expression "having reached the unsurpassable, complete enlightenment" occuring in this (fifth) section we may observe that comparison of all versions of the first section suggests that at the first meeting with the five ascetics the Buddha had perhaps called himself only

[1] The formula "imperturbable is" etc. can also be found in MN 26, but not in connection with the discovery of the four noble truths, only overcoming various kinds of suffering is mentioned. It is first (I p. 167) used by the Buddha and then (I p.173) by the first five disciples (after the intensive guidance indicated in chapter 2).

Tathāgata. It is possible[2] that he also used the epithet *sammāsambuddha* found in the Pāli version (and in MN I p.172) and in Lalitavistara (with equivalents in the Vinayas of the Mahīśāsakas and Dharmaguptakas). But this would not be as significant a term as *anuttaraṁ sammāsambodhiṁ abhisambuddho* in the fifth section, which has an equivalent in all other versions. The idea that this report refers to removing last theoretical doubts does not imply that this was done in a purely theoretical way. The text employs words (and synonyms not mentioned in the above summary) that point to intuition (which, by the way, does not wholly exclude external stimuli[3] and some reflection). If his discovery of the middle way and his first experience are called an enlightenment, we could speak of a second enlightenment or call the enlightenment described in the fifth section a, partly intuitive, explication of his first experience[4].

It is not probable that the Buddha had his first experience of release by the discovery of the four noble truths. But for the theoreticians of the dhyāna path this interpretation seems to have suggested itself after some time and to have led to the claim that one has to realize the four noble truths at the end of this path. Very likely the cause for this development was a non-Buddhist spiritual environment which demanded that one is released only by means of a knowledge or a truth. This demand was perhaps strengthened by the Buddhist method of discriminating insight which, in the meantime fully established, employed concepts and therefore seemed to conform to this demand. In order to meet it the theoreticians of the dhyāna path could base themselves on the above-mentioned report. However it is not wholly suited to the elaborated dhyāna path.

---

[2] Besides the above-mentioned *sammāsambuddha* we find in the second section of the Pāli version *majjhimā paṭipadā tathāgatena abhisambuddhā* (also in the parallel passage in the Mahāvastu). That the Buddha had sought for *bodha* or *sambodha* and had proclaimed that he had found a path that leads to *bodha* or *sambodha* can be found in MN 36 (in the passage quoted in chapter 1, *bodha*) and in the second section of the "first sermon" (*sambodha* is one of the synonyms which describe the result of the middle way). In the Lalitavistara we read in what corresponds to the first section: "I have realized immortality and the way leading to immortality (*amṛtaṃ mayā sākṣātkṛto* [sic] *'mṛtagāmī ca mārgaḥ*), I am enlightened (*buddha*), all-knowing, ...".

[3] Compare note 5 of the Introduction.

[4] The formula "It was not until ... that I maintained that I had reached the unsurpassable, complete enlightenment (and knew: imperturbable is my heart's release ...)" was first used very likely as a part of (and an addition to) the account discussed here. It can be found together with other contents at some other places in the canon. I cannot consider the tenor of these places authentic. Especially AN 8.7.4 seems to be a glaring example of a superficial use of this formula. There we read (abridged): It was not until my knowledge of all heavenly beings was completely pure that I maintained that I had reached the unsurpassable, complete enlightenment and knew: imperturbable is my heart's release, this is my last existence, now there is no longer rebirth. However, I do not exclude that some tenets could be interpreted as additional intuitions of the Buddha.

This path clearly presupposes some practice before one realizes the four noble truths. But the Buddha was, according to the last passage of the fifth section in the Pāli version, released after having discovered the four noble truths; here the fourth truth was not known earlier and could therefore not be practised.

CHAPTER SIX

# THE PREPARATION FOR DHYĀNA IN THE DETAILED DESCRIPTION OF THE DHYĀNA PATH

At several places[1] in the canon a detailed description of the dhyāna-path to salvation is given that differs from the noble eightfold path, not only because of its copiousness, but also because of the addition of new elements (not all of them are found at each place). Some of these new elements will be discussed in subsequent chapters. I should now like to describe the elements which appear to correspond to the noble eightfold path. These elements were already necessary to illuminate the noble eightfold path. I will go into more detail, eventhough I do not intend to strive for a complete rendition. I shall especially emphasize those points which illustrate that the method for reaching dhyāna is not a superficial nor an artificial one, and that consequently, dhyāna could be a profound existential experience.

The beginning of this elaborated path to salvation states (abridged),

> "The Tathāgata, the Arhat, the perfect enlightened one ... appears in the world ... he instructs the world ...(concerning things that he) has experienced and realized himself. He teaches the Dharma (doctrine) ... This Dharma is heard by a householder or the son of a householder ... Having heard this Dharma he puts his trust (*saddhā*) in the Tathāgata. Provided with this trust he thinks, "... living at home it is difficult to lead the completely perfect, completely pure ... religious life (*brahmacariya*). Now then, let me shave off my hair and my beard, put on yellow robes and leave home for homelessness." And thereafter he abandons small or large possessions, a small or large family, he shaves off his hair and beard, puts on yellow robes, and leaves his house for homelessness (*agārasmā anagāriyaṁ pabbajati*)."

This passage can be summarized with the following concepts: trust in the Buddha, the desire to put in practice what one has been taught, the radical decision to abandon possessions and family and to become a religious mendicant. Previously I used this beginning passage to explain the first two steps of the noble eightfold path. In form (Tathāgata is only a name for the Buddha) and content (only trust in the Tathāgata is mentioned and not also the belief in an afterlife and the retribution of deeds which is probable in the term *sammādiṭṭhi*) this passage does show traces of a development.

---

[1] E. g. MN 27, 38, 39 and 112; see Frauwallner 1953, 162 ff.
See note 15 in Schmithausen 1981, p. 204.

The next passage, however, probably reflects very ancient instructions. It contains the following points. If someone has abandoned his home, then

1. he follows the rules of ascetism concerning physical conduct and speech (P. *sīla*, S. *śīla*)
2. he takes care that sensory impressions and (sensual) thoughts do not gain power over him (*indriyasaṁvara*, "control of the senses")
3. he tries to do everything he does in full consciousness or mindfully (P. *sati*, S. *smṛti*)
4. he regularly looks for a solitary place to meditate.

The text gives the following explanation of these four points. In regard to 1), the rules of ascetic conduct, the most important ones are already indicated at the points "right speech" and "right conduct" of the noble eightfold path; the sequence is now different:

one must not kill (nor harm)
one must not take what is not given,
one must not perform sexual acts,
one must not lie,
one must not be rude,
one must not relate something that could cause dissension,
one must not babble nonsense.

These precepts were, in part, already prevalent in the circles that gave rise to Jainism. But there they had another function: the avoidance of actions (*karma*) which were thought to cause a fine dust to enter the soul. The Buddha applies these precepts for something else, a more direct purpose, the realization of a non-sensual happiness. This section on ascetic conduct, which also contains all kinds of rules for a monk's life (which I will not discuss here[2]) along with the above mentioned elementary precepts, ends with, "If he is provided with this noble group of ascetic conduct, he will feel a flawless happiness (*anavajjasukhaṁ paṭisaṁvedeti*) within himself". A similar remark is also found at the end of the second section, "If he is provided with this noble control over his senses (including thought), he will feel a non-sensual happiness (*abyāsekasukhaṁ paṭisaṁvedeti*) within himself. Apparently in this way a characteristic of the first stages of dhyāna, happiness without desire (see chapter one) is being formed. Nothing is said about happiness in the third section (on doing everything mindfully), but here awareness is being formed which is characteristic of the last stages of dhyāna. If one has already formed this

---

[2] Details may be found in E. Frauwallner 1953 p. 164-65. I have used the rejection of gifts (such as uncooked food, women and girls, slaves and slavegirls, goats and scheep, chickens and pigs, elephants, cows, horses, and pieces of land) that are unnecessary or disturbing as an explanation of "right livelihood" in chapter 3.

happiness and this awareness, then one can go to a solitary place and try to eliminate the remaining disturbances and perfect these conditions. If one does not come in happiness and awareness, then being solitary will be of little use and only give rise to fear (cf. MN 4).

One must certainly have a very positive attitude in order to practise ascetic precepts in such a way that a feeling of happiness arises. This is partially possible because each day one has the opportunity to transform the happiness arising from this conduct into meditation (*dhyāna*) and through this to be revitalized.

Another basis for the feeling of happiness coming from ascetic conduct can perhaps be found in the manner in which the above mentioned precepts are presented, i.e., not only as a means to reach one's own salvation, but also to promote the welfare of others. In order to demonstrate this aspect I shall quote a few sentences concerning the elementary precepts from the section on ascetic conduct.

> "After (this person trusting in the Buddha) has left his home ... he no longer harms any living creature, he does not have a stick, he does not have a weapon, modest, full of compassion he constantly thinks of the welfare[3] of all living creatures (*sabbapāṇabhūtahitānukampī viharati*) ... he does not take what is not given ... he is steadfast, trustworthy and does not disappoint people (if he has promised something) ... what he has heard here he does not tell there, so that the people here are not separated (from the people there), and what he has heard there, he does not tell here, so that the people there are not separated (from the people here); in this way he joins those who are separated and confirms those who are joined; unity makes him joyful, unity makes him happy ... he no longer uses rude language; he speaks words that offend no one, pleasant to the ear, friendly, reaching the heart, polite, bringing joy to many people, bringing pleasure to many people...".

The second section, on the control of the senses (including thought), also has as its goal the creation of a feeling of happiness without desire. It is especially concerned with the situation in which the monk walks through a village or city begging for food. The instruction states,

> "If he sees with the eye a form/colour (*rūpa*), hears with the ear a sound, smells with the nose a smell, tastes with the tongue a flavour, feels with his body something tangible, and thinks with his thought a thing (*dhamma*), then he does not hold on to principal marks nor to minor features. He is concentrated on warding off the principal marks and minor features because bad, unwholesome states of desire and dejection could stream into the person who does not constantly control the senses of sight, etc,".

---

[3] The word *hita* appears to cover more than the terms for salvation that I mentioned in the introduction (note 7), i.e., also the welfare of the world. In SN 2.22 we find e.g. *hitam attano* in a context in which good deeds are a prerequisite of the welfare that later in this world comes to the doer of the good deeds.

In general one can do very little to prevent experiencing objects and corresponding thoughts. When begging for food, the monk will avoid exciting events and the busiest places in a village or city, not the village or city itself. The Buddha did not think of immuring himself in a hut and being taken care of by others, as sometimes was the case later on. Most likely he would have rejected such a method. It is not necessary, because here he teaches a method, which is sufficient for the attentive monk to remain undisturbed by sensual impressions and corresponding thoughts. One should not dwell on these impressions and thoughts a moment longer than is necessary to orientate oneself. If one goes too deeply into the principal marks of what is presented, or into minor features, then one cannot avoid the arising of desire and dejection and it will take a long time before these conditions disappear again. Most of the time they have not dissappeared when one comes back from begging and one settles down to meditate. The basis for a condition free from desire and in happiness is no longer present and an attempt to meditate is bound to fail. If one does take care that the impressions and thoughts are not held fast, then one builds up a feeling of happiness because one has conquered the, generally so powerful, impressions and thoughts. In a quiet place this feeling can easily be converted into dhyāna.

In the third section mention is also made of a spiritual activity, doing everything with mindfulness (*sati*), which forms a basis for dhyāna meditation. One is conscious of coming and going, conscious of looking at something or of allowing one's eyes to look around, conscious of bending or stretching one's limbs, etc. One does nothing unconsciously, one never allows the mind to wander away from what one is doing here and now. If we include the control of the senses which was just mentioned above, one is also immediately aware of the next impression and does not remain thinking about the former one. A kind of spontaneous awareness seems to arise through this exercise. This awareness is central for the two last stages of dhyāna. In the description of the third dhyāna the term *sata* is used together with *sampajāna*. In the description of the fourth dhyāna the term *sati-pārisuddhi* occurs.

In the fourth section a description is given of how one looks for a solitary place for meditation after this preparation. One seeks out such a place after one has begged and eaten one's food in the morning. One sits down with the legs crossed, the body straight, and then does something which in Pali is called, *parimukhaṁ satiṁ upaṭṭhapetvā*. This could mean, holding ones attention within a narrow range of vision[4]. A rather

[4] A concrete and significant indication is found in MN 119 (III p. 89): one should now concentrate on breathing.

old, but perhaps not dating from the most ancient period, instruction states that, before entering dhyāna, one should see if there are traces of the five (groups of) states, known as obstacles (*nīvaraṇa*), present and to get rid of them. These states are 1) covetousness, 2) malice and anger, 3) torpor and drowsiness, 4) restlessness and anxiety, 5) vacillation. Suppressing these states is not a purely negative action; for example, it is stated that one should think of the welfare of all living creatures when removing malice and anger.

CHAPTER SEVEN

# THE IMMEASURABLES

A few times in the previous chapter I pointed to the altruistic side of the preparation for dhyāna-meditation. I should now like to discuss a meditative exercise that, in my opinion, belongs to the oldest level of transmission, but which was sidetracked by subsequent developments. I am referring to the "immeasurables" (*appamāṇa*), i.e., radiating feelings of friendship, compassion, joy, and equanimity in all directions without drawing a line anywhere and without omitting any creature.

A well developed feeling of friendship, compassion, joy, and equanimity is called "release of my heart" (*me cetovimutti*) in AN 8.7.3. There this feeling is further identified with *samādhi* and is successively practised together with contemplation, reflection, joy, happiness, and equanimity, states of mind common to the stages of dhyāna.[1] Remember that at the end of the proclamation of full enlightenment (chapter 5), according to some versions, the Buddha states, "imperturbable is my heart's release (*akuppā me cetovimutti*), this is my last existence, now there is no longer rebirth". This is probably a formula even older than that proclamation (cf. MN 26 I p.167 and 173). Just as in the description of the four dhyānas, the word *ceto* (spirit, mind, heart) is used and not the less inclusive term *citta*. The possessive "my" (*me*) is also used in quite an unconcerned manner, whereas conforming to the development of the doctrine, this pronoun does not appear in the other formulas. In AN 8.7.3 friendship, compassion, joy, and equanimity are called "release of my heart"[2]. One could say that they are not called "imperturbable" and

---

[1] The sutta AN 8.7.3 states next that also the fourfold application of mindfulness (*satipaṭṭhāna*) towards the body, the feelings, the thoughts and the (psychic) qualities is *samādhi* (cf. MN I p. 301) and can be connected with respectively contemplation, reflection, joy, happiness and equanimity. It is true that *satipaṭṭhāna* in the fourfold form transmitted to us (e.g. MN 10) is already mixed up with elements of discriminating insight (observation of the five constituents) and liberating insight (observation of the four noble truths), but in the nucleus it represents, or at least prepares, *sati*, the second of the two important aspects of dhyāna which are mentioned in the description of the fourth dhyāna. In the immeasurables the first aspect, equanimity (*upekkhā*), is present; it is the goal of the last and perhaps most important of these meditative exercises.

[2] Not only in AN 8.7.3, but also in DN 13 and 33, MN 127 and SN 20.5. In all these places the word *cetovimutti* is found alone and is not followed, as in other places, by the word *paññāvimutti* ("release by discriminating insight"), which brings another method into play and points to another release of the heart (see also the introductory remarks to chapter 12).

that something more must be added for realizing final release. The question is whether this addition must consist of a higher intensity or of a dogmatic insight.

Let us first look at the formula most used for this exercise. It states (e.g., MN 7):

> "With a heart (*cetasā*) that is filled with friendship, for some time he pervades one direction, (then) a second, a third, a fourth, (then the sphere) above and below, everywhere identifying himself with everything (*sabbattatāya*)[3], for some time he pervades the whole world with a heart that is filled with friendship, that is wide, great, immeasurable, without hostility, invulnerable."

This passage reveals little intention of overcoming the world but seems to be directed towards creating (transitory) feelings in respect to other creatures. In view of this it is not surprising that later on this exercise was considered as a path to the (transient) brahma world (e.g. MN 83 and 99, and DN 13), or as a path to salvation only if followed by liberating or discriminating insight (e.g. MN 7 and 52, AN 11.2.6). But this does not have to be the oldest version of the exercise. I should like to point out that the description of the four stages of dhyāna also does not show an explicit intention of overcoming the world. However, as I hope to have previously demonstrated, the first section of the first sermon made a connection between achieving immortality and the practising of dhyāna. Soon afterwards the doctrine of the four noble truths came into being and these truths distinctly stated that future existences could be avoided by a path which culminated in right Samādhi. This intention of overcoming the world and suffering could also be present latently in a state of dhyāna in which no thinking occurs because the Buddha's efforts (and those of his first disciples) were already constantly directed towards that end. The description which one used as a guideline for the practice of dhyāna only had to meet this intention. It is true that the description of the immeasurables emphasizes other aspects than that of dhyāna but, in my opinion, it can serve this intention in no lesser degree, especially when it is closely linked with aspects of dhyāna and is called *samādhi* as in AN 8.7.3. This *samādhi* may be the same as that at the end of the noble eightfold path and exclusively rely on its own intensity for liberating the mind from craving, not needing to be followed by a formulated insight. Moreover radiating equanimity points in the same direction as the pure equanimity found in the description of the fourth dhyāna, i.e. one has overcome all emotions and thereby also craving. I should like to point out

---

[3] Buddhaghosa (Visuddhimagga p. 256) also has this reading, although, from a systematical point of view, *sabbatthatāya* would have been much more favourable to him.

that more than 800 years later in his Visuddhimagga Buddhaghosa, the famous dogmatic of Ceylonese Buddhism, describes forty meditative exercises among which the four immeasurables. Although these immeasurables do not have a direct relation to the final stage of the path to salvation sketched by him, according to Buddhaghosa they do belong to the very few of the forty exercises which lead to the higher stages of dhyāna which are not neglected in his system. According to book IX the cultivation of the unlimited feelings of friendschap, compassion, and joy leads to the third stage, the cultivation of equanimity to the fourth stage of dhyāna.

CHAPTER EIGHT

# LIBERATING INSIGHT AND THE DESTRUCTION OF THE CANKERS

In chapters 6 and 7 a description was given of the preparation for dhyāna and of another type of meditation similar to dhyāna. These preparations and this type of meditation may not be the most ancient form of the proclamation, but they are hardly deviating from it, and can be connected with the stage of development that the dhyāna movement had at the time of the eightfold path. This stage was followed by the doctrine of the four noble truths and then by a new concept of the Buddha's enlightenment. A consequence of this new concept seems to have been that also the knowledge of the four noble truths was added to the, in the meantime, already more elaborated path culminating in the right samādhi.[1] One now thought that only by concluding this path with this knowledge one could become liberated from rebirth, because now one supposed that only knowledge is finally liberating. It is therefore not only (kinds of) desire one has to be liberated from but also ignorance. This combination of defects came to be called *āsava* (S. *āsrava*) which can be translated as cankers, imperfections, etc.

It is frequently the Buddha himself who is described as following this dhyāna path, that ends in the knowledge of the four noble truths. Here, however, the four noble truths are not perceived in the three ways which are described in the fifth section of the "first sermon", i.e., as such, what could be done with them and that he had already done everything with them. Here, there is no reason for him perceiving three ways; this is a path to salvation in which from its inception one takes for granted that the four noble truths, especially the path, are something long known. In fact it is the path (whether elaborated or not) that is primary, and the disciples are now expected to conclude it in a way which, according to new ideas, was the way the Buddha found enlightenment and (in some versions) release.

One now thinks that the cankers are conquered by a formulated knowledge and this corresponds to the conquering of desire by discriminating insight, i.e. dissecting the person in five constituents and

---

[1] The word *āsava* literally means "influx". Originally it belonged to Jainism where it referred to karma-particles which flowed into the soul and which robbed it of its natural capacities and bound it to rebirth. In Buddhism the word is only used in a metaphorical meaning.

establishing that they are not the self (see chapter 9). In the doctrine of the four noble truths craving is not conquered by a knowledge, but, as is said in the third truth, "by complete detachment, by abandoning and rejecting (the craving), by freedom from and no longer holding onto (this craving)", which is apparently possible through the right samādhi.

In the versions of the fifth section of the "first sermon" where the discovery of the four noble truths is made responsible also for the Buddha's release, nothing is said of the destruction of craving (or of desire, or of the cankers). Now it is stated that the realization of the four noble truths (as well as the "realization of the cankers") destroys the cankers and that thereby one is released. Although the proposition that this kind of knowledge destroys craving (and ignorance) and thereby causes release has probably been made under the influence of the path of discriminating insight, the knowledge mentioned here does not necessarily have the characteristics of discriminating insight, as later it was sometimes interpreted (e.g. in the Abhisamayavāda of the Sarvāstivādins).

This kind of knowledge is generally called *aññā* (see the Arhat formula at the end of this chapter) and not *paññā* (P., *prajñā* S.). The verb corresponding to *paññā* is used though; he knows (*pajānāti*) as it really is "this is suffering", "this is the arising of suffering", "this is the cessation of suffering", and "this is the path that leads to the cessation of suffering". *Pajānāti* is less established as a terminological concept than *paññā*, moreover in some places (MN 4 and 112) *abhijānāti* instead of *pajānāti* is used in the sentence just quoted. Furthermore, the four noble truths are very briefly indicated here so that the sentence obviously added to the explanation of the truth of suffering under the influence of discriminating insight, "in summery, the five constituents which one grasps, are suffering" does not have had to play a role. All this allows for the possibility of applying the concept "liberating insight" instead of "discriminating insight" for the realization of the four noble truths that should take place in the fourth stage of dhyāna. Though this seems to be a literary construction (see outline), the author may nevertheless have thought of something very close to the concept of the right samādhi. In defence of the possibility of a real praxis one might propose that only the experience of salvation is meant by the realization of the four noble truths.

The content of the next part of the transmitted text, in my opinion, only allows to be considered as a literary product; but that does not mean that this part, especially the description of the result, could not be taken as a mirror of living tradition. After the realization of the four noble truths quoted above, the following passage is found, aside from a few variations, in all the places where the elaborated path to salvation is described (see note 1 in chapter 6):

"He knows as it really is "these are the cankers (*āsava*), "this is the origin of the cankers", this is the cessation of the cankers", and "this is the path which leads to the cessation of the cankers". When he thus knows, thus sees, his mind (*citta*) is released from the canker that is (craving for) objects of pleasure (*kāma*), his mind is released from the canker that is (craving for) existence (*bhava*), his mind is released from the canker that is ignorance. As soon as he is released, the knowledge arises: (the mind) is released (*vimuttasmiṁ vimuttam-iti ñāṇaṁ hoti*)[2] he knows, (re)birth is destroyed, the (religious) life has achieved its goal, that which had to be done has been done, there is no beyond after this state of things".

Here, it is no longer only craving that is to be conquered by the path, but also ignorance. Craving appears to be subdivided into craving for objects of pleasure and craving for existence. Furthermore there is a curious imitation of the four noble truths in the realization of the cankers[3]. The concluding soteriological formula may not be as old as the formula which speaks of the imperturbability of release (see chapter 5), but it gained large appeal and was used, among other things, as an explanation of the brief indication of release in the description on discriminating insight (see outline).

The fact that ignorance is included in the cankers can be explained in the following way. As soon as one employs a knowledge against desire (and other emotional factors), one will very likely, at a certain point, try to derive desire from ignorance in order to make such an employment of knowledge plausible; knowledge destroys ignorance and therefore desire. This idea may have arisen after the introduction of the realization of the four noble truths, but also in the movement of discriminating insight. The dependence of desire on ignorance is expressed in the "twelvefold chain of dependent origination" (see chapter 10) which seems to belong to the stream of discriminating insight. But in the doctrine of *āsavas*, ignorance stands alongside two kinds of desire; the reason for its inclusion is not clear. One can only surmise that the two kinds of desire are dependent on this ignorance. Therefore, the twelvefold chain of dependent origination most probably is the origin of this idea.

---

[2] See Schmithausen 1981, 219-220, note 69 for a discussion of the variants of this sentence.

[3] In his contribution to the panel "Earliest Buddhism" of the VIIth World Sanskrit Conference K. R. Norman pleads for a very early incorporation of the term *āsava* into Buddhism. He observes (p.3) that at the end of the elaborated dhyāna path the four statements about misery are not referred to as noble truths and that they (therefore?) could be subordinate to the four statements about the *āsavas*. He thinks that the statements about misery led to a parallel, but inappropriate, set of four statements being evolved about the *āsavas*.

The fourfold realization of the cankers, which imitates the four noble truths, hardly makes a convincing impression (''these are the cankers'', ''this is the origin of the cankers'', etc.). It is difficult to see how this could have had any practical results. Perhaps there was a somewhat edifying effect in regarding the cankers analogous to the four noble truths. At the beginning there may have been an attempt to derive the cankers which consisted of two kinds of craving (analogous to the first truth) from ignorance (analogous to the second truth). Then one could in this way show that the realization of the four noble truths destroys ignorance and thereby the cankers (and consequently rebirth and suffering). Unfortunately in the text transmitted to us the cankers only occur in a set of three (later four) including ignorance; to derive ignorance from ignorance is hardly convincing[4].

In conclusion I should like to comment on the description of the result: If he thus knows, thus sees (i.e., the four noble truths and the cankers analogous to these four truths), his mind (*cittam*) becomes released from the three cankers; as soon as he is released, the knowledge arises ''(the mind) is released'', etc. This became the starting point of the most common description of the Arhat, the person who could be certain that he would never be born again. The formula (already quoted in note 3 of chapter 2) begins with the assertion that an Arhat has destroyed the cankers and ends with the assertion that he became released by right insight (*aññā*). The word *aññā* could be an attempt at distinguishing this knowledge from *paññā* (discriminating insight).

---

[4] See Schmithausen 1981, 205; cf. MN 9 and AN 6.6.9.

# II. DISCRIMINATING INSIGHT

CHAPTER NINE

# DISCRIMINATING INSIGHT

In Vinaya- and Suttapiṭaka we find[1] instructions for reaching liberation from craving and thereby from rebirth by another way than dhyāna-meditation, viz., by discriminating insight (P. *paññā*, S. *prajñā*).[2]

Discriminating insight is knowing that things we normally consider to be the self or belonging to the self cannot be or belong to the self if this self is conceived of as not suffering. To facilitate this "disidentification" the main object of false identification, the human person, is divided into constituents or components; each part is examined as to whether it can be the self and judged as not being the self.

At some places the suggestion can be found that this method, in order to be successfully employed, must be preceded by samādhi which is most probably meant in the sense of dhyāna-meditation, some concentration in examining the constituents being self-evident. The implication of these places is that dhyāna-meditation in order to overcome craving must be followed by discriminating insight. As to dhyāna-meditation this suggestion surely does not reflect the oldest teaching, nor does the locus classicus for discriminating insight, a passage in the Vinaya (I p. 13-14) that acquired the name "discourse on non-self" (*anattapariyāya*), contain a hint at this combination of methods. One could argue that the Anattapariyāya follows the passages called Dhamma-cakka-ppavattana and therefore presupposes dhyāna. But after having presented the ancient tenets of this "first sermon", the Pali-Vinaya compilers tell us that listening to it caused the five ascetics to see that all that originates is bound to be destroyed (not in the content of this sermon) and to become monks

---

[1] For more places than discussed below see Schmithausen 1981 p. 219 note 69 ("... most frequent in SN but seem to be missing in DN and AN").

[2] With this translation of *paññā* I want to indicate the ability and the mental process of distinguishing between permanent and impermanent, suffering and non-suffering, self and non-self. The word *paññā* is also employed in respect to much simpler distinctions, as between *kusala* and *akusala*, *sāvajja* and *anavajja*, etc., e.g. in AN 9.1.5; cf. *prajñāprabhedakuśalās* in section 35 of the longer recension of the Sukhāvatīvyūha which is translated into Tibetan as *śes rab kyis rab tu dbye ba la mkhas pa*. Only at some (very old?) places it seems to have a more general meaning of wisdom, e.g. Sn 881 (there is nothing to be found in the twelfth Aṭṭhakasutta or in the Aṭṭhakavagga as a whole that corresponds with what is described here as discriminating insight). In Vinaya I p. 11 *paññā* follows the words *cakkhu* and *ñāṇa* and precedes the words *vijjā* and *āloka* as a term of the Buddha's enlightenment in regard to the four noble truths (cf. chapter 5), but in the parallel version in the Saṅghabhedavastu (ed. Gnoli I p. 135) *prajñā* is missing.

(i.e., the first members of the Buddhist order). In the Vinaya of the Mūlasarvāstivādins one disciple is related to have become released by hearing the explanation of the four noble truths, but not by meditating (Saṅghabhedavastu ed. Gnoli, I p. 138). This leaves little room for connecting the contents of the "first sermon" with the contents of the Anattapariyāya, which even more unlikely was preached at the first encounter with the five ascetics near Benares than the Dhamma-cakka-ppavattanasutta in the form that is handed down to us. Moreover there are famous Pali sermons, e.g. MN 22 and MN 74 (see below), that teach discriminating insight without any suggestion that it has to be supported by dhyāna[3].

The Anattapariyāya can be taken as the basis of a description of this new method. It distinguishes five constituents of a person, at other places called *khandha* (S. *skandha*):

1. the (material) visible form (*rūpam*)
2. (pleasant, unpleasant and indifferent) feeling (*vedanā*)
3. apperception (*saññā*)
4. dispositions , the only term in the plural, (*saṅkhārā*)
5. perception (*viññāṇam*).[4]

Firstly it states that "visible form", etc. are "non-self" (*anattā*) because if they were the self, they would not lead to affliction (*ābādha*) and one would have ones wish as to visible form, etc.; "thus my visible form, etc., should be, thus it should not be!" (Vinaya I p. 13; cf. MN 35 I p.

---

[3] Cf. Schmithausen 1981 p. 221 and note 71.

[4] The Sanskrit equivalents are *rūpam*, *vedanā*, *saṃjñā*, *saṃskārāḥ* and *vijñānam*. The translation of the three last terms needs some discussion. As to *saṅkhārā*, etymologically it seems to have two aspects, formation or preparation and the thing formed or prepared. It probably points to various volitions and to the dispositions where these volitions come from and which are maintained and strengthened by the actual volitions. In translating I have chosen the aspect of potentiality; see chapter 10 for more discussion of this term.

The terms *saññā* and *viññāṇam* must be considered together. Unfortunately we find no good explanations in the ancient texts. My impression is that they have a similar function and relation to each other as the terms apperception and perception in Leibniz' thought or the terms idea and impression in Hume's concepts. When I translate *viññāṇa* with perception, I have in mind a (not yet interpreting) perception or impression (of colour, sound, etc.) of the senses. The word "consciousness" which is often employed here, is rather inconvenient when one has to interpret *viññāṇam* as a link in the twelvefold chain of dependent origination (see chapter 10) where it seems to point to the first moment of life in the mother's womb. And in as much as "consciousness" suggests that one needs words to be really conscious of a sense perception, this translation is misleading and would be better used for *saññā*. One could argue that the same could be said of "perception" which can be conceived as interpreting perception and is often used to translate *saññā*. But when *saññā* is translated with apperception (or ideation [see chapter 12 note 2]) "perception" for *viññāṇa* is less ambiguous. In connection and opposition to "apperception", "perception" (for *viññāṇa*) can have the clear meaning of not yet interpreting perception. On *saññā* in ancient texts cf. Schmithausen 1981 p. 214.

231). This argument on the constituents not being the self was nearly forgotten in later times.

It was the second argument that became very important (Vin. I p. 14, cf. MN 22 I p. 138-139):

> "What do you think, monks, is visible form permanent or impermanent?—Impermanent (*anicca*), Sir.—Now what is impermanent, is this unpleasant or pleasant?—Unpleasant (*dukkha*), Sir.—Now, what is impermanent, unpleasant (and) bound to change (*vipariṇāmadhamma*), is it proper to regard it in such a way: this is mine, this I am, this is my self (*eso me attā*)?—Surely not, Sir. (What do you think, monks,) is feeling permanent or impermanent? ... is apperception permanent or impermanent? ... are the dispositions permanent or impermanent? ... is perception permanent or impermanent?-Impermanent, Sir.—Now, what is impermanent is this unpleasant or pleasant?—Unpleasant, Sir.—Now, what is impermanent, unpleasant (and) bound to change, is it proper to regard it in such a way: this is mine, this I am, this is my self?-Surely not, Sir."

I shall discuss below the argument used here. Let us first finish the text which now presents the method in a categorical way. Here the constituents appear already to be more than only "one's own" constituents, becoming a kind of elements of the world. The text ends by stating the result of the method.

> "Therefore, monks, whatever visible form there is, past, future (or) present, inward or outward, gross or subtle, inferior or excellent, at a distance or nearby, all visible form should be looked upon with right discriminating insight (*sammappaññāya*) in this way: this is not mine, this I am not, this is not my self (*na mêso attā*). Whatever feeling there is ... apperception ... dispositions... whatever perception there is, past, future (or) present, inward or outward, gross or subtle, inferior or excellent, at a distance or nearby, all feeling ... apperception ... dispositions ... perception should be looked upon with right discriminating insight in this way: this is not mine, this I am not, this is not my self. When a noble disciple, who is learned, looks (upon visible form, etc.) in such a way, he has enough of visible form, has enough of feeling, has enough of apperception, has enough of the dispositions and has enough of perception. Having enough, he frees himself from desire; by being freed from desire he is released.[5] In the released the knowledge arises: (the mind) is released; he understands: rebirth is destroyed, the religious life has been fulfilled, what was to be done has been done, there is no beyond for this state of things."

Having enough of the constituents and thereby becoming free from desire (i.e. craving) is usually connected by later Buddhists with the second argument mentioned above. As to this argument in which "disidentification" comes from being aware of impermanence, let us compare a passage of MN 74 which, in its nucleus, is perhaps older than

[5] The next sentence is an addition. See Schmithausen 1981 p. 219, note 69.

the Anattapariyāya. According to this passage (MN I p. 500) one has to look upon the body, which consists of the four elements, as impermanent, as suffering, as a disease, as an abscess, as a sting, as an evil, as an affliction, as alien, as decay, as empty (*suñña*) [and] as non-self. This series of predicates is confined to an examination of the body. Besides the body only feeling, divided into pleasant, unpleasant and indifferent feeling, is judged, but with slightly different predicates. It is possible that in the beginning only these two constituents (of "one's own" person, not more and not yet of the outside world as well) were examined. At any rate perception was very likely not yet included (see the concluding remarks in this chapter, cf. chapters 10 and 12).

The three kinds of feeling are, like the body, also called impermanent, but then other predicates follow: produced (*saṅkhata*), arisen dependent [on conditions] (*paṭiccasamuppanna*), liable to loss, decay, fading away (and) cessation. It was stated before in this text that one is rid of the longing for the body when one looks upon it in the prescribed manner; it now continues stating: "When a noble disciple, who is learned, looks (upon feeling) in this way, he has enough of pleasant feeling, has enough of unpleasant feeling and has enough of indifferent feeling. Having enough he frees himself of desire; by becoming freed from desire he is released" (etc. as above in the Anattapariyāya).

This instruction in MN 74 is directed to the wandering ascetic Dīghanakha. According to the concluding remarks of this sermon he did not fully take advantage of it; he only grasped an essential point implicitly mentioned in the series of predicates of feeling: whatever is subject to birth (which always is produced by conditions) is subject to destruction. This is called the spotless Dharma-eye. Its effect is that one can apprehend the impermanence of seemingly stable things, when one knows they have ever begun to exist. According to this text the evidence obviously comes from the observation of short-lived feelings where the connection of being produced (by conditions) and being impermanent can be perceived by everyone.

The text also tells us that at the time of this instruction to Dīghanakha Sāriputta stood behind the Buddha fanning him. The thought occurred to Sāriputta that the Buddha has taught that one rids oneself of various things by fully comprehending them. And thinking this over (*paṭisañcikkhato*) [but not by reaching genuine dhyāna, which is impossible, when one stays in the company of others and is fanning and not sitting quietly] his mind without clinging any further, became released from the cankers.[6]

[6] For the description of Sāriputta's release the terminology of "liberating insight" (see chapter 8) is employed: he is released from the cankers. This corresponds with the

Let us now return to the Anattapariyāya and concentrate on its second argument. It is restricted to three predicates (impermanent, suffering and "not one's self")[7] for the five constituents. These predicates are not merely enumerated (as they are found in MN 74 along with other predicates pertaining to the body). Here the first is the logical basis for the second and the second for the third. This is presented as if it was self-evident, but it is not, not only in our understanding of what corresponds in Western languages to these words, but also in the normal usage of these terms in Middle Indic or in Sanskrit. Many persons have experienced "themselves" as suffering; suffering has not precluded them from using the word "self". And many persons have enjoyed things they knew to be impermanent; seeing impermanence has not precluded them from calling things pleasant.

However, the connection between the suffering and "non-self" can be understood, when "self" is taken in an ontological sense as known from passages of the Upaniṣads. This is a historical remark and does not mean to say that the method, as such, presupposes the belief that such a non-suffering self does exist. It uses "self" only in a negative formula: what is suffering cannot be the self (in the text it is asked "can this be my self?" and stated "this is not my self").[8] On the other hand, this negative formula is doing a little bit more than only saying that we are not destined for suffering. In order to say this it employs the word self in a meaning which is not everyday usage, exclusively combining it with non-suffering.

Therefore, we may assume some influence on this method by Upaniṣadic passages or by a background common to both this method

---

remarks of the compilers of the Vinaya at the end of the Anattapariyāya. However, neither in MN 74 nor in the Anattapariyāya the method of discriminating insight itself contains the term *āsava*. In both texts we find two descriptions of the result obtained, of which the second seems to have originated from the elaborated dhyāna path (see outline), but perhaps from an earlier stage of its development, when it not yet employed the term *āsava*.

[7] More precisely, not mine, not I, not my self, but not (as in the first argument) non-self (see next note).

[8] In the first argument *rūpam*, etc., are called non-self (*anattā*). Comparing this with the second argument we can be fairly sure that, at the beginning, this only meant that rūpam, etc., are not (my) self. This would be one of the cases, occurring in Middle Indic and Sanskrit, where the predicate absorbs the negation and the sentence seems to assert something but does not. Cf. Saṅghabhedavastu (ed. Gnoli I p. 138), *rūpaṃ bhikṣavo nātmā*, but later in the sentence, *rūpam anātmā*.

All important passages which use the term *anātmā* can be found in chapter 11 of the thorough study of J. Pérez-Remón *Self and non-self in early Buddhism* (The Hague-Paris-New York, Mouton Publishers, 1980). I do not deny that in some of these passages the term *anattā* is employed rather inflexibly, but this points, in my opinion, to a development of using the shortest term and not, as Pérez-Remón thinks, to the acceptance of an entity non-self which must presuppose an entity self.

and these passages. The best instance for such a passage might be Bṛhadāraṇyaka-Upaniṣad III 7. There Yājñavalkya speaks of a self (*ātman*) which is immortal and controlling all elements and organs from within, never being the object of these elements and organs. At the end he states, "what is different from the [self] is painful (*ārta*)". This last sentence or a similar assertion could have been the model for the connection of suffering and not being the self.

If one was guided by a standard that suffering implies not being the self in order to distance the constituents as not being the self, then one had to also be sure that the constituents inevitably bring suffering or are themselves suffering. The first assertion ("inevitably bring suffering"), used in the first argument of the Anattapariyāya, is convincing when connected with the first noble truth; the five constituents have then to be taken as a term for existence. The second assertion ("the constituents are themselves suffering") is not self-evident and seems to imply some ontological thinking as well. It is argued that the constituents are suffering because they are impermanent. This is convincing if one understands suffering (*dukkha*) as unpleasant in the sense of failing to satisfy the hope for permanency and unchangeability. This hope may be in everyman, but in order to be activated and used in a path to salvation, it seems to need some spiritual background not to make it a pure frustration. We may assume that one would not lay stress on impermanence and unsatisfactoriness if one did not think one knew a way out of the problem, i.e. by giving up identification with impermanent things, not by expecting a change in the nature of things. In Buddhist dogmatics one was fully aware that one had to distinguish between different meanings of "suffering" (*dukkha*), actual suffering and unsatisfactoriness[9]. But these meanings are also connected to each other and therefore we can accept that the first noble truth was not only explained by birth, old age, etc, but also by the constituents as such, which is apparently a later addition.

After presenting the passages which later were called Anattapariyāya, the compilers of the Pali Vinaya state (I p. 14) that while this exposition was spoken by the Buddha, the minds of the five ascetics who had become monks were totally ("without further clinging") released from the "cankers" (*āsava*) (cf. Saṅghabhedavastu ed. Gnoli p. 139). In the Anattapariyāya itself we had already found a statement (in fact, two statements cf. note 5) concerning release, but not from "cankers").

All these statements point to a purely practical aim of this method even in the time of compilation. One is advised to use it in order to be rid of

[9] Later three kinds of suffering are distinguished. See L. Schmithausen, Zur buddhistischen Lehre von der dreifachen Leidhaftigkeit, *ZDMG* Suppl. III, 2, 1977, 918-931.

the identification with the constituents and consequently to be freed from desire and to be sure of not being born again. Neither here nor in most other places in the Vinaya- and Sutta-piṭaka which describe this method do we find a theoretical discussion on the existence or non-existence of the non-suffering self, which is the standard used in distancing the constituents.[10] At a very few places it is related that a question about a "self" was put to the Buddha, but that he declined to give an answer.[11] Nevertheless the Abhidharma and post-canonical literature of most Buddhist schools contain the conclusion that in the Anattapariyāya and similar places the existence of a self as such, and not only the constituents being the self, is denied. Modern scholars, as well, feel obliged to express an opinion on this matter. Most of them follow the Buddhist non-self tradition, but a few think that the existence of a self is presupposed in these sermons.

To have a view (whatever it may be) in this matter distinguishes Buddhist tradition and modern scholars from an ancient, purely practical, approach where such questions were thought to be an obstacle to spiritual progress and where it was not considered problematic to leave matters undecided. Leaving such questions undecided is a remarkable feature in view of the history of ideas in India, as well as in Europe, and can, perhaps, be explained by the influence of a strong personality who, as is told of the Buddha, only wanted to achieve salvation. This influence would have lasted for some time even after his death because not only ancient layers of the canon show this abstention in theorizing about the self, but almost the whole collection of Vinaya- and Sutta-piṭaka. On the

---

[10] In my opinion Pérez-Remón (see note 8) has convincingly shown that in Vinaya- and Sutta-piṭaka (with the exception of some texts as the Parivāra which was composed in Ceylon) a denial of the existence of a self cannot be found, only a denial of things being the self. But I do not follow his opinion that this fact and the positive use of the term *attan* in other passages *must* be interpreted as presupposing a notion of the real existence of a (personal) self. This would only be right if the the Buddha and his first disciples had consented to the principle of the excluded middle which allows one to interpret a negation (in this case, not deying the existence of a self) as assertion of the contrary (i.e. the existence of a self).

[11] E.g. the Ānandasutta SN 44.10 (IV p. 400). The Buddha is asked by Vacchagotta, "does a self exist?" and remains silent; then he is asked, "does a self not exist?" and again he remains silent. Thereupon Vacchagotta goes away. After this report the sutta describes a dialogue between the Buddha and Ānanda which can be interpreted as already showing some inclination to deny the existence of a self. The Buddha is represented as saying that he did not agree to the question proposing the non-existence of a self, because he was afraid of causing bewilderment (the suggestion probably being, if he had *truly* told him that a self does not exist). With L. Schmithausen (*ZMR* 1973 p. 177, note 52) we may consider this dialogue a later addition to the report on Buddha's silence. Cf. also MN 2 (I p. 8) where the Buddha expressly rejects the opinion that "my self" exists as well as the opinion that "my self" does not exist.

other hand it is only natural that, given the absence of strong spiritual guidance, the formulations used in this method evoked speculation on the existence or non-existence of a self. I think that this standard of distancing the constituents cannot be understood without knowing some assertions of the Upaniṣads and I do not exclude the possibility that, of the frequent, mostly reflexive, positive usage of the term "self" outside this method, some sentences may point to Jain ideas about the self/soul (not unchanging, or non-suffering, but essentially perfect and obliging to remove defilements from it). But I shall not myself enter into the discussion whether the method of discriminating insight requires the existence or non-existence of a self, a discussion which is frustrating because there are not enough philological data on this point. In my opinion, this is no accident, but in line with the intention of a purely practical aim.

Here I merely want to say a few words about the fact that the majority of Buddhist tradition has chosen the theory of nonexistence of a self. We have nearly no documents on the beginning of this matter, so most of what I shall say about the possible development is a guess. The best explanation seems to me that in this matter speculation did not begin with advocating the non-existence of a non-suffering self (besides the constituents), but with rejecting the theory of a so-called "person" (*pudgala*) as an entity which is suffering and obtains relief from going on a path to salvation. A certain Vātsīputra (flourishing around 300 B.C.?) is said to have taught this theory. Looking only at the *word* "person" in the sense of an individual self, we cannot call this an innovation. Many canonical passages speak of a person or (one's) self, which must achieve something, must be developed, purified, guarded, etc. But while this is obviously everyday, though existentially relevant, usage (most of the cases neither showing a conscious use of a convention, as the traditional deniers of a self assert, nor pointing to a soul, as some modern scholars think), Vātsīputra seems to have had a metaphysical entity in mind. We may suppose that such a theory was thought necessary by persons who, after some time, wanted a theoretical, not only an existential, motivation for going on a path to salvation, especially the path of discriminating insight, which does not allow answering the question who benefits from it. However, if one considers just this method of discriminating insight, then a serious problem arises which could have led to rejecting this theory of a "person" and, as a corollary, to devaluating the existentially relevant canonical passages about a person or (one's) self which must achieve something. This problem is that one judges the constituents with the standard of a self which is unchangeable and non-suffering and that a personal self obtains relief, i.e. would change from suffering to non-suffering, by practising this method.

These two selves cannot, logically, be identical. As the constituents (most certainly including perception at this stage of the development) comprise everything known of a person, it is not only difficult, but utterly impossible to separate "a person" from them. These five constituents are ever changing and supposed to definitely stop at the death of a person devoid of craving. The conclusion must therefore be that there is no person or self who achieves salvation.

As soon as the theory of a person or individual self reaching salvation was rejected by asserting the non-existence of a self, there was little chance for waiving the same verdict for the unchanging self. But this seems, at least in the beginning, more a matter of terminology. Many Buddhists believed that there is an unchanging and non-suffering entity called nirvana, but they did not want to connect it with the term self which, outside the abovementioned method, is mostly employed in respect to a suffering self. This usage does not only contain longing for salvation, but also, and much more, the wish to survive and to enjoy oneself as an individual, which is the very cause of suffering.

When I explain the origin of the negation of the existence of a self as a "logical" reaction to the theory of a "person", I do not exclude the possibility that already at the beginning of this negation or shortly afterwards, some persons (as in later times) thought that this approach was necessary to safeguard the praxis of discriminating insight. In later times the tenet of the non-existence of a self was in the first place defended by pointing to the undesired consequences of the contrary theory on the aim of being wholly freed from desires. It was admitted that a method similar to discriminating insight could be practised with some success even by a person who believed in the existence of a self. But this would not lead to final success, because this belief prevents a person from eradicating subtle forms of egoism which can be the root of new desires.[12]

[12] This is taken from Dharmakīrti's polemic against the contemplation of suffering (*duḥkhabhāvanā*) as recommended by early Nyāya writers who, in this matter, obviously were inspired by Buddhism, but did not want to give up the idea of a personal self, regarding it as necessary for motivating a person for employing such a method to gain release. Dharmakīrti's position is that it is better not being able to theoretically motivate a person, but showing the real path to salvation than the other way around; you cannot have it both ways (see T. Vetter, *Der Buddha und seine Lehre* ... Wien 1984, 28-30 and 126, note 1). Compare the opening lines of the ninth chapter of the Abhidharmakośa, an essay devoted to refuting the idea of a personal self. All impurities binding man to rebirth originate, as these lines say, from the idea of a self. A very lucid description of the *anattā* doctrine as a strategy in "mental culture" in Theravāda Buddhism is given by S. Collins in his book *Selfless Persons: Imagery and thought in Theravāda Buddhism* (Cambridge, University Press, 1982). The only objection I have to this book is that Collins, like a Theravāda "theologian" too easily synthesizes various canonical utterances, projecting the Theravāda position into Vinaya- and Sutta-piṭaka and sometimes simply identifying these with the Buddha's word. But even on canonical passages one can find stimulating discussions of words and sentences in this book.

Such an extra motive would explain why the majority of Buddhists has chosen the non-self theory which is an analytical approach to this problem. Given the loss of a nondogmatic attidude, it seems the best dogmatic framework to preserve what the Buddha taught.

In regard to theoretical motivation for practicing the path the deniers of the existence of a self were clearly aware that this was not possible. The only way would have been to consider the constituents as the self to be benefited by the destruction of the same self at the moment of final release. There is a verse, cited in Visuddhimagga (p. 436), that shows that one was conscious of this fact and had learned to live with it, "Only suffering (exists), no [person] who suffers. There is no agent, only an action. Nirvana exists, [but] no person who is [to be characterized as] extinguished. A path exists, [but] there is no [person who is] going [on it]."[13]

In the first stage of the method of discriminating insight there probably was not such a big gap between praxis and theoretical motivation. "Perception" seems not yet to have become a constituent to be judged as non-self. It functioned as the centre of a person and as the entity that transmigrates (see chapter 10). It corresponded to an individual soul in other schools, but was not referred to as such (the first attempts to do so perhaps led to its consistent incorporation into the transient constituents, cf. MN 38). And it was not considered to remain in an isolated and perfect state at the time of release. As a passage in MN 22 (p. 140) states, "when the gods ... search for (the perception of) the (dead) monk whose mind is released, they cannot find [it] [so that they could say], the perception (*viññāṇam*) of the thus-gone (*tathāgata*)[14] is supported by this. Why? Already in this life I call a thus-gone unknowable." The same passage continues by stating that annihilation is certainly not the goal of the Buddha's teaching. This may point to a period when one tried to avoid affirmation as well as negation in this matter (see chapter 11). But we have one place (the concluding verse in DN XI, see chapter 12) where perception is described as having no attributes, being endless (*ananta*) and radiating all around. In early times some persons might have considered individual perception dissolving into this great perception at the time of release.

---

[13] A similar statement can be found in vers 192 of the Pramāṇasiddhi-chapter of Dharmakīrti's Pramāṇavārttika.

[14] This passage is clear evidence that in the earliest period the word *tathāgata* was not used only for the Buddha. Here it is a released monk who is referred to by this term.

CHAPTER TEN

# THE TWELVEFOLD CHAIN OF DEPENDENT ORIGINATION

The principle that all that comes into being is dependent on certain causes and prerequisites and that one may avoid undesirable situations which are not directly avoidable by searching out and overcoming the causes and prerequisites is already connected with the doctrine of the four noble truths. Suffering arises from craving. By following the eightfold path one can conquer craving and thereby suffering.

In Vinaya I p. 40 it is reported that Assaji, one of the five ascetics who had become the first disciples of the Buddha, condensed the doctrine of the Buddha into the following formula by which he converted Sāriputta and Mogallāna.

> "The Tathāgata has stated the causes as well as the cessation of the situations/mental states (*dhamma*) that arise from causes; this is what the great ascetic proclaims[1]."

In later times this abstract formulation was held in high esteem by many Buddhists and served as a kind of creed.

A removable cause or prerequisite often does not immediately precede a result. What lies between that distant cause and the effect one wants to avoid can also be part of a diagnosis. Thus a series of causes and effects arises. The following series is very simple: craving brings forth a new existence, and a new existence is subject to old age and death.

In canonical texts we find various chains of causes/prereqisites and consequences. I shall direct my attention here to the series known as the twelvefold chain of *the origination* of suffering *dependent on* certain conditions (P. *paṭicca-samuppāda*, S. *pratītya-samutpāda*), beginning with ignorance. This series gained the most influence in Buddhist thought.

In chapter 8 (on liberating insight and the destruction of the cankers) I assumed that the new element of ignorance was included in the doctrine of the three cankers (two kinds of craving plus ignorance) in order to give a better explanation of the destruction of craving by liberating insight; insight destroys ignorance and thereby the craving which depends on ignorance. But the doctrine of the three cankers does not explicitly mention that craving is dependent on ignorance. One does find this mentioned in the twelvefold chain of dependent origination. I had to postpone discuss-

---

[1] *ye dhammā hetuppabhavā tesaṁ hetuṁ tathāgato āha / tesaṁ ca yo nirodho evaṁvādī mahāsamaṇo.*

ing this series because the dependence is described in such a way that it seems improbable without the introduction of discriminating insight; four links of this chain are referred to by terms we know as designations of the constituents towards which this method is directed.

In Udāna I 1 this series is presented as follows[2]:

> "If the one exists, then the other exists; from the origination of this that originates, viz. from
> 1. ignorance (*avijjā*) as a condition (-paccayā)
> 2. the dispositions (*saṅkhārā*) arise [i.e. are activated]; from these as conditions
> 3. perception (*viññāṇaṁ*) arises; from this as a condition
> 4. name and visible form (*nāma-rūpaṁ*) arise; from these as conditions
> 5. the six sense organs (*saḷāyatanaṁ*) arise; from these as condition
> 6. contact (*phasso*) arises; from this as a condition
> 7. feeling (*vedanā*) arises; from this as a condition
> 8. craving (*taṇhā*) arises; from this as a condition
> 9. clinging (*upādānaṁ*) arises; from this as a condition
> 10. existence (*bhavo*) arises; from this as a condition
> 11. birth (*jāti*) arises; from this as a condition
> 12. old age (i.e. decay) and death (*jarā-maraṇaṁ*), distress, lamentation, suffering, dejection, and disturbance (*soka-parideva-dukkha-domanass-upāyāsā*) arise. Thus is the origin of this whole mass of suffering".

There is also a negative formulation of this chain which makes the purpose of this series more clear (Udāna I 2). It states that ignorance is the condition that one must eliminate in order to eliminate suffering:

> "If the one does not exist, then the other does not exist; by eliminating the one, the other is eliminated, namely by eliminating (1) ignorance the (2) dispositions are eliminated; by eliminating the dispositions, (3) perception is eliminated ... by eliminating (11) birth, (12) old age and death are eliminated etc. Thus this whole mass of suffering is eliminated."

Except for *saṅkhārā* (see below) I have tried to translate all terms as literally as possible. Without much explanation one sees that all the emphasis is put on eliminating ignorance and one quite easily also understands some of the links (e.g. that old age and death are dependent on birth). But other connections remain obscure (e.g. why does percep-

---

[2] For more canonical places see F. Bernhard, Zur Interpretation der Pratītyasamutpāda-Formel, *WZKSO* XII-XIII (1968) 53-63, and E. Lamotte, Conditioned Co-production and Supreme Enlightenment, *Festschrift for Walpola Rāhula*, 119-132.

Bernhard (following E. Waldschmidt) shows how, in different texts, this chain was discovered by the Buddha first after his enlightenment, then together with his enlightenment, and finally became the only content of the enlightenment. Lamotte also points to passages where this chain is known (long) before enlightenment (p.121-123), but refuses any attempt at ordering the different statements historically. In his opinion "... we must allow ourselves to be guided blindly by the canonical sources".

tion arise from dispositions?), and the series as a whole makes a very puzzeling impression.

The best way to promote comprehension seems to me to first isolate the last part of the chain from "craving" up to "old age", etc., which is easy to understand. This is an elaborate version of the second noble truth or, in the negative formulation, of the third noble truth; only the term "grasping" could (but need not) show some influence of a new development, viz. if thereby grasping the constituents was meant. This part can be interpreted as follows: craving is, by causing grasping, the origin of a new existence which, after roughly nine months, becomes manifest by birth after which the various kinds of suffering are difficult to avoid; by overcoming craving one escapes all these consequences.

Now the links before "craving". The literal explanation must regard them as a sequence of conditions for craving as tradition also regarded them. This is convincing in the case of ignorance, because in regard to a chain which begins with ignorance and contains craving, we may assume that craving is no longer the condition of suffering to be directly destroyed (by means of the "right samādhi"), but that ignorance has become this condition, and that discriminating or liberating insight are now recommended as the real means to gain salvation.

The problem, however, is that the philologist as well as the traditional commentator arrive at an interpretation of the first two terms (ignorance and dispositions) of this sequence as conditions belonging to an earlier existence (see below). The whole sequence would then be a too complicated manner to teach that craving is dependent on ignorance. Literally it states that our ignorance in this life will predispose us for craving in the next life which inevitably leads to another life as insight can be of no help then. To avoid this undesired conclusion Buddhist commentators have claimed that "craving" also means "ignorance" (and "ignorance" also "craving").

The historian is allowed to seek a solution which does not strain terms in such a way. It seems obvious that two different chains of dependent origination of suffering were superficially combined into the twelvefold chain. The first part (links 1-7) is a more developed attempt at explaining the origin of suffering than the second part. It will be shown that it contains, in a new terminolgy (also occurring as the designation of a constituent), the dependence of craving (included in *saṅkhārā*) upon ignorance. In this respect the addition of the last part (8-12) is apparently superfluous. But this addition can be understood as motivated by apologetics. The purpose of explicitly stating the dependence of "craving" (old term) and its consequences upon ignorance and its consequences would then be to criticize those persons who proclaimed that they had overcome craving by the "right samādhi". They may have overcome craving, but not only through "right samādhi". Even if they are unconscious of this fact, they must have also used a kind of insight without which, to an adherent of discriminating or liberating insight, it seems impossible to destroy craving once and for all. This motive would also explain why the last part was not properly adjusted, craving (and grasping) remaining the only condition(s) for the rebirth described at the end of the chain.[3]

In order to connect the two chains the last link of the first part, probably suffering, had to be brought under the general term "feeling", which is usually divided into pleasant, unpleasant and indifferent feeling. The link with craving is convincing if one thinks of pleasant feeling as its condition. Unpleasant feeling may also lead to craving, but can just as well bring us to our senses.

Let us now try to explain the details of the first part of the twelvefold chain. "Contact" with objects (6) is a condition for "feeling" (7). And for this "contact" (6) the six sense organs (5), including the mind, are needed. The "six sense organs (5) are based on "name and form" (4) which is an ancient Indian term for "person". It originally expressed that the name of a person is also essential, but for the Buddhists it hints at a (viable) combination of the four psychical constituents ("name") and the physical constituent ("form") of a person.

What is described in the conditions 7 up to 4 is valid for every situation in life. But the chain, dealing, most likely, with rebirth and having special temporal aspects, is probably expressing the following idea at this point: as conditions of contact with objects the six sense organs cannot start to function fully before the moment of birth. They may be seen as the result of the growth of a person ("name and form") in the mother's womb.

In interpreting "name and form" as the main part of the life in the mother's womb we follow the suggestions of some traditional commentaries (e.g. Abhidharmakośabhāṣya III 20-21). If we are right in doing so, we may also expect that its condition "perception" (3) points to a special time in life. Concurring with the same tradition we may take it as the beginning of life in the mother's womb.

---

[3] Some shorter chains of dependent origination could be interpreted as a reaction to this suggestion. E.g. SN 35.106 accepts that craving is dependent on feeling, and feeling on contact. But it expressly states that by eliminating craving through complete absence of desire (*taṇhāya asesavirāganirodhā*)—not by eliminating feeling, etc., as the twelvefold chain has it—grasping is eliminated, and thereby existence, and thereby birth, and thereby old age and death.

But why should this point be called "perception"? A very simple answer can be given to this question. This is a relic of an ancient idea that "perception", as the subtlest part of a person, is the transmigratory entity. At some places in the canon we still can find instances of this idea, e.g., when after the death of Godhika, Māra is seeking the "perception" of this monk (SN 4.23). "Perception" as a condition of "name and form" would then mean the moment when "perception" has entered the mother's womb (cf. DN I p. 63 *viññāṇaṁ ... mātukucchismim okkamitvā*) and a new life begins with "perception" as its centre.

But we must be cautious. This part of the twelvefold chain, though showing traces of old ideas, probably presupposes discriminating insight at a stage where "perception" was considered transient as well. In this sense the monk Sāti is rightly criticized in MN 38 for stating that it is always this same "perception" which transmigrates (*sandhāvati/saṁsarati*). But what the author/compiler of MN 38 suggests instead as the true meaning of perception is too much of the other extreme. In his opinion perception arises dependent on eye and (visible) form (and nothing more), on ear and sound (and nothing more), etc. He arrives at a purely materialistic view of the origin of perception and can never explain the third link of the chain as conditioned by *saṅkhārā*.

If under these circumstances one wishes to explain "perception" as the starting point of a new existence, as suggested by the canonical remark cited above (DN I p. 63, "perception" has entered the mother's womb), one has to assume that at the very moment of "entrance" at least one sense (that of touch), based on "name and form", must be (faintly) working. This seems to be the reason why at some places[4] in the canon we find a chain of the same conditions as in the twelvefold chain, but ending in "perception" as a condition of "name and form" and in "name and form" as a condition of "perception", both being mutually dependent on each other. The sequence of conditions here is forced to turn back, as it were, and does not go on to dispositions and ignorance, thus ending in conditions which cannot be destroyed by insight or by samādhi and being a purely theoretical scheme in this respect.

However at most places "name and form" are simply dependent on "perception" (and not vice versa). This appears to be the more ancient form of linking, just because it is so difficult to understand for the developed actualistic thinking on perception.

This form of linking suggests a more substantial view on perception. In a general sense it means that for actual perception not only organs of sense and objects are needed, but also the presence of the constituent

[4] E.g. SN 12.67 (see chapter 11) and DN 14 (II p.32).

perception. As to "perception" as the third condition in the twelvefold chain one must assume that after death, the constituent perception continues to exist without the support of sense organs and therefore in a latent state. Entering the mother's womb it is again activated however faintly and is, as such, the starting point of a new life.

That the moment when the transmigrating constituent perception has entered the mother's womb is meant by the third link in the chain may be supported by Abhidharmakośabhāṣya III 21c, where "perception" is explained as a name for the moment when the five constituents[5]—in this system a bundle of fives streams of momentary entities—have entered the mother's womb. Originally neither a set of five constituents nor a theory of streams of momentary entities seems to have been connected with this link. But it is very probable that, given the name of the third link, perception was thought of as transmigrating (perhaps accompanied by faint feeling, apperception and emotions). This perception was seen as a kind of substance, though not (or, no longer) as unchanging. In the next chapter I want to show how one tried to avoid the extremes of eternity and annihilation, of identity and difference without already having theories on the causality of a "stream". A kind of theory is the use of the image of a seed which can be found at some places in the canon (e.g. AN 3.8.6); just as under certain conditions a seed grows into a new plant without becoming a totally different thing, so too does perception develope into a new life.

Let us now turn to the second link in the twelvefold chain, *saṅkhārā*. This is a difficult word, etymologically coming close to "states/things being formed or prepared [to do something in the future]". If we are right in supposing that the five constituents play a part in this chain, we may expect that the meaning of *saṅkhārā* is not too far from the meaning of *saṅkhārā* as a constituent. The Śālistamba-sūtra, a sermon transmitted in Sanskrit, fulfills this expectation the best. According to this text the *saṃskārāḥ* of the twelvefold chain are desire, anger and confusion in regard to objects (*rāga-dveṣa-mohā viṣayeṣu*)[6]. Though the sermon as a whole does not seem to belong to the oldest strata of Buddhist literature, this interpretation may be fairly old (just as its central image of perception as a seed of rice); in any case, it is not the interpretation which later commentators support (see below).

*Saṅkhārā* as a condition of "perception" which is conceived as the first moment of a new existence must belong to a period before this moment. We can think of actual emotions in the former life preparing the consti-

---

[5] *matuḥ kukṣau pratisandhikṣaṇe pañca skandhā "vijñānam"*.

[6] Mahāyāna-sūtra-saṃgraha, part I, ed. P.L. Vaidya, Darbhanga 1961, p.103,19.

tuent perception for a future existence *and* of dispositions maintained or strengthened by these emotions which, after death, cause perception to seek a new place for reincarnation. Both aspects might have been meant, but they are not clearly distinguished.

Though apparently more than only desire and also (etymologically) having an aspect of latency, *Saṅkhārā* can be equated, in function, to craving in the scheme of the four noble truths. There are places in the canon where this equation is obvious. In MN 64 (I p. 436) the aim of religious life is described as the cessation of the *saṅkhārā*, the giving up of all *upadhi* (acts of "adding", clinging), the destruction of *taṇhā* (craving), *vi-rāga* (absence of passion), etc.

Most traditional commentators explain *saṅkhārā/ saṃskārāḥ* as karma ("deeds" having a result not directly experienced, and the latent energy laid down by those deeds which finally produces the result) when it occurs in this context. In order to provide the same conditions for birth at the end of the chain they also explain *bhava* (10, "existence") as karma. This interpretation reflects the penetration into Buddhism of a kind of thinking that in the time of the Buddha was represented by Jainism. All our (morally significant, in each case, all selfish) deeds must be repaid after some time without a single exception. Therefore in this view deeds are a cause for rebirth, not only for the quality of a new existence, *if* one is reborn by craving, as was the oldest Buddhist position, or by ignorance and craving, as is the more advanced Buddhist position represented in the first part of the twelvefold chain.

For Buddhism this did not have such practical consequences as were the attempts to overcome all karma by self-castigation in Jainism. There was a theoretical solution to this problem. Karma needs other factors such as ignorance, desire, hatred, etc., which were called *kleśa*, to be able to effect rebirth. A person who has destroyed the other factors need not try to dissolve his store of karma in order to become released.

The identification of "bhava", the tenth term of the twelvefold chain, with karma can be seen as a mere convention. But it must be admitted that the term *saṅkhārā/ saṃskārāḥ* is susceptible to acquiring such a content. It shares with karma the same verbal root *kṛ* (to do). Furthermore, its aspect of potentiality (etymologically as "things which are formed and prepared [to do something in future]") allows one to think of growing attachment as a result of indulgence in some passion[7]; and this is a kind of retribution (though not precisely the same as was connected with the thinking on karma). The equation becomes most convincing when karma

---

[7] In another context than that of dependent origination of suffering the term *saṅkhārā* could be used as an explanation of positive moral, intellectual and artistic dispositions.

is reduced to intention (*cetanā*)[8], the assumption being that it is intention that makes an action a "deed" which has invisible future results. The emotions (desire, etc.) which lead to rebirth and can lead "to deeds" which determine the quality of a future existence are now[9] replaced by intentions to act which are coloured by emotions. The emotions themselves, whether they directly cause deeds or colour intentions to act, are now according to Abhidharmakośa III, 21 to be included in the first term of the twelvefold chain, "ignorance".

After having discussed *saṅkhārā*, there remains one link, ignorance, to be explained. Without some kind of ignorance *saṅkhārā* cannot arise and lead to a new existence. If we are right in assuming that a motive for introducing the twelvefold chain was to defend discriminating (and liberating) insight against an older method, then ignorance would be the opposite of discriminating (or liberating) insight and would mean the absence of insight in the tranciency, etc. of all things (or the absence of the knowledge of the four noble truths).

In course of time one was no longer satisfied with the mere absence of insight as a condition of the *saṅkhārā*. Ignorance had to be conceived as a real force. This favoured the move of the emotions from *saṅkhārā* to ignorance mentioned above. All these forces were given the name *kilesa*, S. *kleśa*, which means "impurity". One of the first attempts to make ignorance a real force can be found in Sn 730, where ignorance (*avijjā*) is called great confusion (*mahā-moha*) in the context of a chain of dependence similar to the twelvefold chain. "Confusion" is obviously taken from the series of terms desire (*rāga*), anger (*dosa*, S. *dveṣa*) and confusion used above as an explantion for *saṅkhārā* and originally, like anger, conditioned by desire rather than being its condition.

This verse in which ignorance is explained by confusion is part of a sermon (in the Suttanipāta) having its centre in Sn 728. The latter is apparently much older, and "... persists ... as an oasis amid scholastic accretions" as Lord Chalmers (Suttanipāta XVII), rightly describes it in my opinion. There we can find in a nutshell what seems to be the original intention of the twelvefold chain :

---

[8] The canonical passage mostly cited in this connection is AN 6.6.9 (III p.415): *cetanāhaṁ, bhikkhave, kammaṁ vadāmi/ cetayitvā kammaṁ karoti—kāyena vācāya manasā*. In chapter 14 I hope to demonstrate that this is not the oldest position. Besides, not even this passage reduces karma to only intention. It is intention *and* what actually comes forth from intention.

[9] This equation cannot be found in the Abhidharmakośa III 21b and the direct prose commentary (here *saṃskārāḥ* are the good and bad deeds of an earlier existence which now bear fruit), but it occurs in the prose commentary after III 24, which is a kind of appendix to the explanation of the twelvefold chain, probably representing the opinion of the Sautrāntika school.

> "... A dull person who, ignorant, produces "adding" (*upadhi*, cf. above; not in the sense of a substratum, but of craving), again and again goes on to suffering. Therefore, having insight (*pajānam*), one should not produce "adding", seeing that from birth comes forth suffering."

Later, however, another purpose of this chain began to dominate, the description of all important causes and stages leading to and forming a part of existence. The main import was the beginningless causal continuity of existence, sustained by man himself and not by (a) god. In Chinese Hua-Yen tradition it became dependent co-origination and as such the central idea of a more than analytical worldview.

CHAPTER ELEVEN

# NO COMPLETE DESTRUCTION

The death of a released person was soon considered a noncontinuation of all five constituents including perception (*viññāṇaṁ*). This strongly suggested total annihilation (much more than the passage cited at the end of chapter 9 where the gods cannot find the perception of a released person). But to think of total annihilation obviously was too contrary to what one knew of the intention of the Buddha. There are passages in the suttas where, by means of the four positions (*catuṣkoṭi*), a formally interesting defence is made against this consequence. The four positions are the following four possible answers to a question: 1) A, 2) non-A, 3) A as well as non-A, 4) neither A nor non-A. By denying all four possiblities in the case of the continuation of the existence of one who is released (A = exists after death) one wants to reject every theory as being irrelevant. This is the first theme I should like to discuss in this chapter. The second topic of this chapter is closely connected with it. The method of discriminating insight emphasizes the impermanence too much. But it is exactly the continuation into a next existence of what is after some time called the constituents that since ancient times formed the starting-point from which one embarked upon the path to salvation. After the rise of discriminating insight, the aspect of continuity was reestablished in the theory of dependent origination. One could now ask what is the relation between a transient thing and its effect which seems to be a continuation of the thing? Are they different as all other things are different, or identical? Here also the four positions offered some help. But now the fourth position is presented in such a weak way that the negation of all positions does not eliminate a positive meaning of neither A nor non-A.

In the first theme the four possibilities negated are 1) the one who is released[1] exists after death (*hoti tathāgato parammaraṇā*), 2) the one who is released does not exist after death, 3) the one who is released exists as well as does not exist after death, 4) the one who is released neither exists nor does not exist after death. Perhaps in this case points 3 and 4 are no possibilities at all and, consequently, do not have to be negated. But examining this need not be the task of one who wants to avoid every formulation of theory by using these negations. It is sufficient that he knows

---

[1] See chapter 2, note 2.

other cases in which points 3 and 4 are significant; in order to take no risks he may also negate these points here. Point 3 is significant where one can imagine a differentiated answer. Taking an example from the history of Buddhism we see that according to some schools the world is both finite and infinite. It is finite in respect to its expansion above and below and infinite in so far as immeasurable universes exist on the same level as ours (Abhidharmakośabhāṣya III 3, towards the end; cf. DN 1 I p. 23). In respect to point four probably one originally thought of the negation of two concepts which represent the extremes of a line; the negation puts us in the, as yet, nameless middle point of the line (cf. the middle way in chapter 2). "Neither A nor B" would have been more correct, than "neither A nor non-A". But even the latter construction managed to result in accepted language usage. In the next chapter we will be introduced to a state of meditation called "the sphere of neither apperception nor non-apperception". What seems to be meant is a state that is at the brink of non-apperception (for a more original meaning see Appendix). In my opinion only by interpreting it as a middle way can we make the fourth position significant and, consequently, a significant object for the negation aiming at rejection of all theories, which is another "neither-nor". In DN 2 (I p. 58) Sañjaya Belaṭṭhiputta tries to avoid every theory by rejecting all four positions in relation to a) the existence of a future life (*atthi paraloko*), b) the existence of beings spontaneously appearing (*atthi sattā opapātikā*), c) the existence of the fruit (i.e.) result of good and bad deeds (*atthi sukatadukkaṭānaṁ kammānaṁ phalaṁ vipāko*), and d) the existence after death of one who is released (*hoti tathāgato param-maraṇā*). In the context of these terms he avoids the positive, the negative, the complementary and the medial position (cf. DN 1 I p. 27). This attitude has been criticized. Such criticism is understandable because according to the doctrine of the noble eightfold path one must be distinctly convinced of certain things ("right views"). A belief in the points mentioned under a), b), and c) most certainly belongs to these things (see chapter 3, note 3). Most probably in ancient times even the belief in the existence after death of the one who is released was part of right views because in the above-mentioned sections of DN 1 and 2 (which seem to be much older than the suttas as such) point d) is discussed in the same way as points a) to c).

But in MN 63 in the presence of a certain Māluṅkyāputta a distinction is made between things that have not been explained by the Buddha (*abyākata*) and those that have been explained by him (*byākata*). The possibility of the existence after death of one who is released appears here along with the questions whether the world is perpetual or not perpetual, infinite or finite, and whether life/soul (*jīva*) and the body are identical or different. All these things are considered not to have been explained by the Buddha; only the four noble truths were explained by him. A reason is also given as to why the Buddha did not discuss the above mentioned questions. This would not promote salvation, on the contrary it would hinder it. If someone would only begin to follow the path to salvation after he had been given an answer to these difficult questions, he could be compared with a man who has been hit by an arrow, but refuses medical help until he knows who shot the arrow, what kind of bow was used, etc. He would die before all his questions had been answered.

In MN 72 it is reported that the Buddha in answer to Vacchagotta's questions, which were the same questions left unanswered in MN 63, stated: I am not of the opinion (*na ... evaṁdiṭṭhi*) that the world is perpetual, that the world is not perpetual, etc., (the first three questions only appear in the affirmative and the negative position but the question of the existence after death of one who is released shows all four positions. An explanation of the always negative reaction follows. Opinions (*diṭṭhigatam*) are not things on which to dwell or to be concerned with; they are themselves full of suffering and do not make an end to suffering as such. The text then turns to the path to salvation via discriminating insight into the constituents and consequently lands in the situation where the cessation of the constituents at the death of one who is released suggests the total annihilation of a person. Apparently in order to avoid such a suggestion, i.e. with a different motive than mentioned in MN 63, the question of the existence after death of one who is released is asked again (in a slightly deviant and more elaborated form). Questions put in the affirmative and in the negative form, in the as well as form and the neither-nor form are said to be not appropriate. In MN I p. 486 the following words are ascribed to the Buddha (abridged):

> I myself no longer have an opinion, as I have seen (*diṭṭham*): thus is visible form, thus the arising of visible form, thus the disappearance of visible form; thus is feeling ... thus apperception ... thus the dispositions ... thus perception, thus the arising of perception, thus the disappearance of perception. That is why the Tathāgata has been released because he has destroyed all illusions (*maññita*), all disturbances, all inclinations (*anusaya*) towards saying "I" and "my" and towards arrogance.
> Vacchagotta questions, Where does a monk whose mind is so released (*vimuttacitta*) come into being (after death)? "Come into being" does not apply. So does he not come into being? "Not come into being" does not apply. Then does he come into being as well as not come into being? "Come into being as well as not come into being" does not apply. Then does he neither come into being nor not come into being? "Neither come into being nor not come into being" does not apply. Vacchagotta says that he no longer understands anything and that he is now completely confused. The answer to this is: This is deep (*gambhīra*), difficult to penetrate,

peaceful, exalted, not accessible to reasoning (*atakkāvacara*), subtle, comprehensible only to the wise. For you who have other opinions and interests this is difficult to understand. Because of this I shall ask you a question: What would you think? If a fire should burn before you, would you then know, a fire burns here before me? Yes, I would know this. If one should ask you now: On what basis does this fire burn before you, what would you then answer? If I was asked this question, I would answer, this fire before me burns on the basis of grass or wood. If the fire before you should extinguish, would you then know: the fire before me is extinguished (*nibbuta*)? I would know this. If one should now ask you: the fire before you which is extinguished, in which direction did it go, to the east, to the west, to the north or to the south, what would you then answer? This does not apply. This fire, that burnt on the basis of grass or wood, is only called extinguished because the fuel has been burnt and there is no more fuel available. Exactly in the same way, Vacchagotta, visible form, feeling, apperception, dispositions and perception, by which one could designate a Tathāgata, are now given up and once and for all uprooted. Now a Tathāgata can no longer be designated by them; he is now deep, immeasurable, unfathomable as the great ocean. "Come into being" does not apply, "not come into being," does not apply, "come into being as well as not come into being" does not apply, "neither come into being nor not come into being" does not apply.

Looking back at the three places which are quoted in connection with the negation of the four positions concerning the existence after death of one who is released we can establish the following points. In DN 2 the use of this formula is criticized (probably because one was convinced that there is an existence after death of one who is released). In MN 63 this formula is included in the questions which the Buddha did not want to discuss, only the four noble truths are important. In MN 72 the method of discriminating insight appears and now this formula is used by the Buddha himself in order to avoid the opinion that the one who is released is annihilated. In the example of the extinction of the fire[2] is clearly shown that what really ends is the fuel which is comparable to the constituents, not the fire which is comparable to the one who is released. The latter can no longer be designated and is therefore called "extinguished". The same is said by "a Tathāgata ...is now deep, immeasurable and unfathomable as the great ocean"[3].

[2] Frauwallner (1953, 226) gave convincing evidence that the example of the extinguishing of fire in ancient India does not suggest total annihilation. See also F.O. Schrader, Die Fragen der Königs Menandros, Berlin (1907) p. 153 note 137.

[3] Another sutta (SN 22.85; the speaker is Sāriputta) attacks the ideas of a certain Yamaka, who holds that he whose cankers are destroyed ceases to exist after death, by also pointing to the intangibility of a Tathāgata. It states however that one who is released is already incapable of being grasped here and now. He is not identical with, nor different from the constituents, nor is he to be determined as being in the constituents.
Cf. MN 22 I p. 140: I call one who has thus gone (*tathāgata*) not to be found already in this life.

The four positions are also applicable to the second question which cannot be avoided in connection with the rise of discriminating insight: what is the relation between a transient thing and its effect which seems to be a continuation of the thing? Here one must also avoid undesirable theories, but now in such a way that a certain degree of theory is possible. The predicate "transient" makes the concept "perpetual" an impossibility when used in conjunction with the constituents. But is "transient" itself absolutely valid? Apparently not, because the constituents have a continuity which only terminates at the moment of release.

Suffering defined as the five constituents and the unpleasant experiences connected with them is, according to the description of dependent origination, continuously produced and producing and consequently not eternal, i.e. not remaining identical with itself. But it is also not just arbitrarily transient, so that what follows could be considered something completely different. A particular consequence can only exist as the result of a particular thing previously existing. Is it possible to describe this causality by means of a combination of identity and difference ("A as well as B")? Here this seems to result only in a contradiction. Or is the negation of both identity and difference a good, or at least the best possible, description? This seems feasible, but only if identity and difference are not eliminated in such a way that this can be used to support the view that everything originates by chance. I will illustrate this problem by means of two suttas.

The first sutta, SN 12.17, describes how Acela-kassapa asks whether suffering 1) is caused by itself, 2) is caused by another[4], 3) is caused by itself as well as by another, 4) is caused neither by itself nor by another, but originates by chance. The Buddha is said to have answered no to all four questions. But this does not mean that no suffering exists. An explanation of the negations follows. If the same [person] causes [suffering] and undergoes [it] as well (*so karoti so paṭisaṁvedayati*), then it is the position that suffering is caused by itself and that implies something eternal (*sassata*). If the one [person] causes [suffering] and the other undergoes [it] (*añño karoti añño paṭisaṁvedayati*), then it is the position that suffering is caused by another and that implies annihilation (*uccheda*). Eternity and annihilation are extremes. Avoiding both extremes the Tathāgata pro-

[4] The words *sayaṁkataṁ* and *aparaṁkataṁ* (in the fourth position *-kāraṁ* is used instead of *-kataṁ*) probably come from a simple query whether that which one experiences is caused by oneself or another (cf. the explanation given for the rejection of all four positions in SN 12.17). In the two suttas cited here it is however only applicable to the subject of the sentence, suffering (SN 12.17), old age and death, etc (SN 12.67). The reason behind this is probably to avoid any allusion to a person who is something other than a phase in dependent origination.

claims the teaching by means of the middle (*majjhena tathāgato dhammaṁ deseti*) doing so with the words, "from ignorance as a condition the dispositions [arise], from the dispositions as a condition perception (arises)", etc.

We see that the sutta arrives at a theoretical middle way. Only two positions which must be avoided are mentioned at the end, caused by itself and caused by another. This points to the fourth position (caused neither by itself nor by another). Apparently there was no other way to handle the situation if one wished to theoretically sustain the description of dependent origination of suffering. However it is amazing that in the passage previous to the one just mentioned all four positions are rejected. There is, it is true, no contradiction to the earlier negation of the fourth position, because that was formally incorrectly interpreted (neither caused by itself nor by another means that it exists by chance and that, of course, must be rejected). But it is curious that the middle way chosen later was not utilized earlier as the fourth position and not rejected. Tradition may play a role in this case; one was perhaps accustomed to the rejection of everything included in the four positions. There is also the possibility that one wanted to attack a theory of random origination.

The second sutta I wish to discuss continues the argumentation of the first sutta (SN 12.67; Mahākoṭṭhika puts the questions, Sāriputta answers). Analogous to the four questions described above it is asked in connection to specific terms of the series of dependent origination (see chapter 10) whether they are caused by themselves or by another. Are old age and death caused by themselves or by something else, etc.? Is birth caused by itself or by something else, etc.? Is existence caused by itself or by something else, etc.? Etc. The answer is: old age and death are not caused by themselves, they are not caused by something else, they are not caused by both themselves and something else, they are not caused neither by themselves nor by something else [in the sense that they] originate by chance. And still old age and death [arise] dependent on birth. A similar answer is given in relation to the terms previous to this one in the series of dependent origination; each time it ends with a sentence containing "and still" (*api ca*): and still birth [arises] dependent on existence; and still existence [arises] dependent on clinging etc., etc.

The questions and answers cease with the term perception. Here we do not find: and still perception [arises] dependent on the dispositions, but: and still perception [arises] dependent on name and form, even though previously is was stated that name and form [arise] dependent on perception. The sutta also states that perception and name and form support one another as two bundles of straw leaning against one another. If one succeeds in knocking down one of the two, then the other will fall down and all things that are supported by the two bundles. If one succeeds to eliminate perception or name and form (it is not said how this could be done; by living in a dark cave? by suicide?), then the other will be eliminated, as well as the remaining conditions of dependent origination.

However our interest here is not aroused by the rather curious beginning of the series[5] (which is again substituted by a beginning in ignorance at the end of the sutta). I only wish to point out that in questions and answers the traditional concepts of dependent origination (up to perception) are brought together in a kind of relation which one could refer to as a theoretical middle way.

I interpret this as, old age and death (and all the other terms in the series) are not caused by themselves, cause and effect are not identical. Old age and death are also not caused by something else—something that has nothing to do with them—cause and effect are not completely different. Old age and death are not caused both by themselves as well as by something else, because this is a contradiction and aspects under which both a positive and a negative description could be given are not visible. Finally old age and death are not caused neither by themselves nor by something else, in the sense that they could arise at random. In this way it appears as if one has maintained the usual rejection of the four positions. But one is not radical enough in rejecting and can not be so, as long as one's aim is to explain causality. The fourth question and answer are formulated in such a way that the possiblility of forming a kind of theory in terms of a middle way is left open. This allows for the possibility of "and still" in: and still old age and death [arise] dependent on birth. If the fourth position in a formally incorrect manner contains random origination, then it must be rejected, but it is not rejected as such; old age and death (and consequently the remaining terms of dependent origination and in the end, all things) originate from a specific cause, but cause and effect are neither identical nor different.

---

[5] My opinion on the possible motive for the formulation of this series can be found in chapter 10. The argument that it must be earlier than the twelvefold chain because it is so curious fails to convince me.

# III. SPHERE-MEDITATION

## CHAPTER TWELVE

# A MORE ARTIFICIAL FORM OF MEDITATION

In the last two chapters we had to concern ourselves with theoretical issues which were largely the result of the introduction of discriminating insight. Discriminating insight is a means of conquering desire and other cankers and, thereby, ending rebirth. The imperturbable (*akuppa*) release of the heart, an important component concerning life here and now in the most ancient doctrine is no longer mentioned in this context[1]. But there are a few suttas (e.g., MN 119 at the end) which speak of a release of the heart (*cetovimutti*) without the designation "imperturbable". Furthermore they state that by destroying the cankers a pure release of the heart consisting of a release by discriminating insight may already be obtained in this life (*āsavānaṁ khayā anāsavaṁ cetovimuttiṁ paññāvimuttiṁ diṭṭhe va dhamme sayaṁ abhiññā sacchikatvā upasampajja viharati*). This is convincing to a certain degree, because the detachment which arises through discriminating insight does not only hold for the period after death, but also has a liberating influence on the present life. But this is not the imperturbable and all-encompassing release of the heart which may be associated with the original dhyānameditation and the practice of the immeasurables (chapter 7).

We may assume that there were some persons who did not accept this as sufficient. They, too, no longer had access to the old dhyāna-meditation, but they knew of states of meditation (originally practised by non-buddhists), that culminated in a cessation of all apperceptions and were impervious to physical suffering. They perceived a means of making these states accessible by adding them to a system, not precisely the old system, of four stages of dhyāna.

There were four states of meditation which were considered accessible after having gone through four stages of dhyāna:
1. the sphere of the infinity of space (*ākāsa*),
2. the sphere of the infinity of perception (*viññāṇa*),
3. the sphere of nothingness,
4. the sphere of neither apperception (*saññā*) nor nonapperception.

Not much information is found on these spheres (*āyatana*) which are devoid of apperception of visible form, but in certain passages so much

[1] One can however find a combination of the terms *akopya*, *cetovimukti* and *prajñāvimukti* in the Lalitavistara (ed. Lefmann p.418) and the Mahāvastu (ed. Senart p.333).

is said that one gets some idea of the procedure. For example in MN 111 (III p. 27), "...by overcoming in every way apperception of visible form (*rūpa-saññā*), by the cessation of [all] apperceptions concerning something that offers resistance (*paṭigha-saññā*), by not paying any attention to apperceptions of multiform [things] (*nānatta-saññā*) one reaches and remains for some time in the sphere of the infinity of space (i.e., in the apperception) "space is infinite"; ...by overcoming in every way the sphere of the infinity of space one reaches and remains for some time in the sphere of the infinity of perception (i.e., in the apperception) "perception is infinite"; ...by overcoming in every way the sphere of the infinity of perception one reaches and remains for some time in the sphere of nothingness (i.e., in the apperception) "there is nothing"; ...by overcoming in every way the sphere of nothingness one reaches and remains for some time in the sphere of neither apperception nor non-apperception."

When I state that one can get some idea of the procedure in this way, then I am referring to the transition from the apperception of visible and diverse forms to the simple apperception of the infinity of space, as well as the transition (via the infinity of perception) to the even more simple apperception of nothingness. It also seems understandable that then a "sphere" follows in which there is hardly any possibility of apperception ("neither apperception nor non-apperception"). But it is not clear how one reaches this last stage; and the sphere of the infinity of perception, which lies between the sphere of the infinity of space and the sphere of nothingness, is also a puzzle.

I shall first deal with the problem of the infinity of perception. The meditation of the spheres probably originated in non-buddhist circles. It is possible to find a reason for the conception of the sphere of the infinity of perception. In connection with this reason some light is cast on an artifical dhyāna-meditation which should be seen as the prerequisite to the transition to the meditation of the spheres. The second problem, the transition from the sphere of nothingness to the sphere of neither apperception nor non-apperception, is more difficult. It is not clear what one thought of this matter in the period of the adoption of this kind of meditation. When it does begin to be clear, we are already in a period of relatively younger suttas and we are also confronted with an additional stage after the sphere of neither apperception nor non-apperception, i.e., the cessation of (all) apperceptions and feelings (*saññāvedayita-nirodha*).[2] I

---

[2] I do not wish to imply here that the cessation of apperceptions and feelings is as young as these suttas. I have not mentioned this state before because the concept that this state should follow the sphere of neither apperceptions nor non-apperceptions ap-

shall base my description of the transition to the last stage on these later suttas and on the Visuddhimagga. Here we find a rather successful assimilation of the climax of an originally non-Buddhist meditation, an assimilation which seems to reflect practice although in most of the texts it is probably no more than a literary theme.

The curious stage of meditation known as the infinity of perception becomes more understandable when one takes into account that in some passages in the canon (e.g., MN 112, III p. 31 or SN 18.9) a doctrine of six elements is mentioned. In this doctrine the usual four elements, earth, water, fire and air are followed by space and perception. In general these six elements are considered to be transient, unsatisfactory and non-self just as the five constituents. But in one passage (DN XI at the end) perception is placed far above the four gross elements and is considered invisible and without bounds (*ananta*, cf. MN 49, I p. 329).[3] This statement corresponds to some descriptions of the great self or the Brahman in the Upaniṣads (e.g. Bṛhadāraṇyaka II 4 12 ...*idam mahad bhūtam anantam* ... *vijñānaghana eva*, Taittirīya II 1 ...*satyaṃ jñānam anantam brahma*). If we look in the Upaniṣads for a relation between the great self and the elements, then we find, in the Taittirīya (II 1), the concept that first space [or ether] (*ākāśa*) arises from this self (*ātman*), then air arises from space, then fire from air, then water from fire, and finally earth arises from water (and plants, food, and human beings arise from earth). Parallel to this concept of evolution we also find in the Bṛhadāraṇyaka (II 4 12: *etebhyo bhūtebhyaḥ samutthāya tāny evānuvinaśyati*) traces of a doctrine where perception—the animating element—clots in creatures, composed of other elements, ("arises for these creatures") and dissolves again in the great element perception, when the creatures dissolve (in the other elements). In this doctrine one can be assured of immortality, but

---

pears to be a development within Buddhism itself. Compare the concluding remarks in the Appendix.

With the translation of *saññā* as "apperception" instead of "ideation" I want to express that a state without *saññā* seems to be more than only having no ideas; it seems to be a state in which one is not distinctly aware of any object. On the other hand, *saññā* (and *sañjānāti*, see a passage quoted below in this chapter and compare note 9), when used in respect to attempts to reach such a state of mind, includes also having abstract ideas and thoughts of an object not present (for everyday usage compare chapter 9 note 4). With regard to the first meaning Schmithausen (1981), usually following R.E.A. Johansson's suggestion "ideation", speaks of a clear and definite consciousness or apperception of the object (p.214 note 51) and (p.227 note 100) of a distinct (i.e. ideative) consciousness.

[3] It is also striking that in DN 2 (I p. 76) and MN 77 (II p. 17) the body is called transient by means of four synonyms, whereas, in contrast, the *viññāṇa* present in the body is not called transient (cf. SN 55.21).

no individuality remains after death and one has no apperception of one's immortality (*na pretya saṃjñāsti*)[4].

If we know that "perception" has both an individual as well as a cosmic aspect, then it becomes clear why it can appear infinite; it is infinite in its cosmic aspect. Perhaps we may also regard space and perception as a kind of cosmic sheaths encompassing the other elements. But when Buddhism incorporated the meditation of the spheres, "perception" was no longer the highest entity which had nothing superior to it. The sphere of nothingness surpasses the sphere of infinite perception. Moreover Buddhists were thinking especially in terms of stages of meditation as is apparent from the succeeding sphere of neither apperception nor non-apperception. Consequently the questions whether a particular "sphere" objectively corresponds to something and what that something precisely is would not play such an important role.

If it is correct to presume that the spheres of the infinity of space and of perception are based on the doctrine of six elements, then one would expect to find traces of meditation on the gross elements, too. One can, indeed, find them in the "Kasina spheres" (P. *kasiṇāyatana*, S. *kṛtsnāyatana*, perhaps literally: the sphere of a unit) mentioned in some passages of the old canon (e.g. MN 77 II p.14 or AN 10.3.5.) and being the centre of meditation in the most respected summary of the Theravāda tradition, the Visuddhimagga. In ancient times there were ten Kasinas: earth, water, fire, air, blue, yellow, red, white, space, and perception. As one can see, four basic colours have been put in between the four gross elements and space and perception.[5] According to the old formula one was supposed to conceive each of the ten Kasinas as being "above, below, and around, undivided and immeasurable" (*paṭhavīkasiṇam* [etc.] *eko sañjānāti uddhaṁ adho tiriyaṁ advayaṁ appamāṇaṁ*). As far as conceiving an object as immeasurable is concerned this appears to be similar to the exercises found in chapter 7 on the "immeasurables" (but not in regard to the state of the heart). But in the Visuddhimagga we no longer find that a Kasina sphere is considered as being immeasurable. It is even characteristic of the technique that one first concentrates on a limited piece of clay (a smooth disk), a limited amount of water (in a saucer), etc., and by starting from this one passes through various stages of dhyāna. Infinity only becomes a topic when one has reached the fourth stage of dhyāna by this method and wishes to go on to the spheres of

[4] See P. Thieme, *Upanischaden*, Ausgewählte Stücke, Stuttgart (Reclam Universal Bibl. 8723) 1971, 70-77.

[5] See AN 10.1.6-7 and AN 11.1.7-9 for meditations which use a series of six elements without the four colours.

meditation which are devoid of all visible form. Infinity is only associated with space and perception. Each of the ten Kasinas is now employed to generate dhyāna. Therefore, the Visuddhimagga is consistent in substituting the last two instances of the old Kasina series, space and perception, by concentration on (a limited amount of) light and a limited space.

I shall now proceed to the second problem mentioned above, the transition from the sphere of nothingness to the sphere of neither apperception nor non-apperception. Most texts, considering the latter state lying at the border of apperception, mention still another (complete) cessation of apperceptions and feelings (*saññāvedayita-nirodha*); of course the problem of transition touches this stage to a greater degree. The "cessation of apperceptions and feelings" probably did not originally belong to the spheres devoid of all visible form and is a Buddhist innovation. Presumably at one time the sphere of neither apperceptions nor non-apperceptions was meant to be the same thing.[6] The name "neither apperception nor non-apperception" probably had a more radical meaning (see Appendix). By some persons this state was criticized as not leading to salvation. This critique had gained a place in the biography of the Buddha and had become known in this way.[7]

Probably in a period already dominated by the method of discriminating insight some persons wished to make use of this wasteland and discovered in the cessation of apperceptions and feelings a state (or rather a name) not yet touched by any criticism. "Neither apperception nor non-apperception" now becomes the last but one stage and its description is to be understood as a middle way formulation allowing for a more radical negation of apperceptions. In this way one could express one's striving for a release of the heart[8] that is more than the detachment through discriminating insight and which, as some assume, here and now

---

[6] See Bronkhorst, *Two Traditions*, 77.

[7] This refers to the famous episode in which the Buddha before his enlightenment reaches the sphere of nothingness when he is with Ārāḍa Kālāma and the sphere of neither apperception nor non-apperception with Udraka Rāmaputra, but does not become released. Philological arguments (see Bareau 1963, 13-27; Bronkhorst, Two Traditions, 80) bring the authenticity of the story into doubt.

[8] The terms "release of the heart without *nimitta* [object of apperception]" (*animittā cetovimutti*) in MN 43 and " concentration of the heart without *nimitta* " (*animitto cetosamādhi*) in MN 43 and 121, DN 16 (II p. 100) and AN 6.6.6. (III p. 397) apparently mean the same or almost the same as the cessation of apperceptions and feelings. But this release of the heart is obviously not the same as the one originating in the ancient dhyāna-meditation.

brings one in touch with the nirvana lying beyond all changing psychic states.[9]

Presumably all attention was originally directed towards a reduction of apperceptions[10]. It was probably also taken for granted that this reduction would arrive at a point where a conscious attempt of reducing would have a contrary effect and that, here, habit had to take over the task of conscious attempts. But there is little or no information found on this point in the ancient texts. When we do find some information, it is in apparently late (parts of) suttas. Here we detect a somewhat different method which is evidently influenced by discriminating insight. These passages, however, are also not clear enough and that is why I think it permissable to call upon evidence in the Visuddhimagga. Although this work was written roughly 400 A.D., in my opinion it has preserved the method influenced by discriminating insight very well.

In the Parinibbāna-sutta (SN 6.15) and at the end of DN 16 we find the first inklings of an opposition to a relatively smooth transition to a state devoid of apperceptions. Calling upon Anuruddha, who was considered to be an authority on the supernatural, the last minutes of the life of the Buddha are described. Here the Buddha, perhaps according to an old tradition, enters the final nirvana from the fourth stage of dhyāna. But before he does so, he reaches the cessation of apperceptions and feelings, and this comes about in a curious way. First he enters the first dhyāna, then, contrary to the ancient descriptions, he abandons it; then he reaches the second stage of dhyāna and abandons it. The same description is given for the third and fourth stage of dhyāna. In the same way he proceeds to the spheres of the infinity of space, the infinity of perception, nothingness, and neither apperception nor non-apperception. This last sphere is also abandoned and then the Buddha enters the cessation of apperceptions and feelings. This state is also abandoned and then the entire series is back-tracked until he again reaches

[9] So very clear in chapter 23 of the Visuddhimagga (ed. Warren/Kosambi 1950 p. 607): ... *diṭṭhe va dhamme acittikā hutvā nirodhaṁ nibbānaṁ patvā* ...
In this context one might also mention the statement in AN 6.5.4 (III p. 356) that those who meditate (*jhāyin*), in contrast to those who are devoted to the doctrine and who use discriminating insight, stay in a state in which they touch the sphere of immortality with their bodies (*amataṁ dhātuṁ kāyena phusitvā viharanti*): compare the article "Musīla et Nārada" by L. de La Vallée Poussin, *Mélanges chinois et bouddhiques* 1936-1937, 189-222. But this could also refer to the original dhyāna-meditation.

[10] One could refer to a place in DN 9 (I p. 184). There a monk who has reached the sphere of nothingness—the most extreme point of apperception (*saññagga*)—thinks: it is better that I no longer think; if I continue to think, I have every chance that I will lose these [subtle] apperceptions and that again gross apperceptions will arise ( ... *acetayamānassa me seyyo / ahaṁ ceva kho pana ceteyyaṁ ... imā ca me saññā nirujjheyyuṁ, aññā ca oḷārikā saññā uppajjeyyuṁ*).

the first stage of dhyāna. From this stage he again proceeds upward, each time abandoning a state before entering the next one, until he reaches the fourth stage of dhyāna, which he abandons; then he enters the final nirvana.

What the reason is for the continuous entering and abandoning of meditative states may become clear if we look at MN 111. This is a rather theoretical sutta and I am referring to it only because of a lack of a better source. But it does carry traces of a practice which later, in chapter XXIII of the Visuddhimagga, is described much more convincingly. The traces lie in the judgement of each stage of dhyāna and each sphere (the sutta mentions instead ten to fifteen psychic qualities in these states) as arising and then passing away and in the assertion that there must be a release beyond this. Only in regard to the cessation of apperceptions and feelings (combined with discriminating insight, see below) the sutta says: there is no release beyond this. But the rationale for this is missing in the sutta, because here this state also has (now no longer specified) psychic qualities and these are also judged to be arising and passing away. The author of this sutta, which is presented as a description by the Buddha of the capabilities of Sāriputta, states only at the sphere of neither apperception nor non-apperception that one must first leave this state before one is capable of judging the qualities, which he no longer specifies, attributed to this sphere. If he had been a little more attentive, he would have mentioned the process of first leaving a state and then judging it already at the first stage of dhyāna. It is certainly not possible to observe, as is stated in the text, the disappearance of these qualities in any of these states, because they are constituted by these qualities. It is also difficult to understand how one would be able to specify the qualities of the second stage of dhyāna onwards and judge these qualities to be transient, while being in these states which are without contemplation and reflection. In spite of the careless construction, in my opinion, this sutta clearly points to a tradition in which meditation must continuously be interrupted in order to be observed with discriminating insight; by doing so, one becomes detached from this stage.

It is stated in the Visuddhimagga that he who only practises meditation can at the most reach the sphere of neither apperception nor non-apperception. But one who combines meditation with the discriminative judging of each different stage of meditation acquires the habit of abandoning each meditative state. This habit enables a person to leave the sphere of neither apperception nor non-apperception without a conscious effort, and consequently, enter the cessation of apperceptions and feelings.

In the Visuddhimagga the cessation of apperceptions and feelings is a state characterized by the lack of psychic processes and cannot be thought of in terms of arising and passing away. The discriminative estimation of the preceding stages justifies, to a certain degree, identifying this cessation of apperceptions and feelings with nirvana. This state is said also to raise one above every form of physical suffering and not only above psychic suffering as in the case of detachment. In the Visuddhimagga an Arhat and an Anāgāmin are capable of reaching the cessation of apperceptions and feelings. An Anāgāmin is someone who has destroyed the causes of rebirth in the lower spheres of the world, does "not come back" to these spheres; he is reborn in higher spheres and from there enters nirvana. Consequently in the Visuddhimagga the discriminating insight used to reach the cessation of apperceptions and feelings is not a means of destroying rebirth, neither is this state of cessation itself a means. It rather appears to be that only those who have discriminating insight to a great degree and who, in addition, possess a talent for this kind of meditation will be able to reach the cessation of apperceptions and feelings.

But what was the connection of this state to the search for salvation in ancient times when this way of meditation apparently was not yet combined with discriminating insight? At the end of some suttas (e.g. MN 25 and 26) after the description of reaching the state of cessation, we find the obscure formula, "after he has seen with discriminating insight, his cankers are completely destroyed". (*paññāya c'assa disvā āsavā parikkhīṇā honti*). Probably the best interpretation of this formula is that one did not only consider the state of cessation as an end in itself, but also considered it to be a means of releasing oneself from rebirth. In order to communicate this to the adherents of discriminating insight, they formulated their conviction of also being released from rebirth in the jargon used by their opponents; the cankers are now destroyed and if you know only a destruction by discriminating insight, they must have been destroyed by this.[11]

One could propose that together with the first traces of the use of discriminating insight as a means of reaching a state of cessation, one also finds the judgement that this state itself is arising and passing away (MN 111, see above, and MN 121) and that this could be a good explanation of the obscure formula, i.e., realizing the transientness of even this state one is released from all cankers. I do not deny the possibility of this ex-

[11] This formula following the assertion that a person has reached the state of cessation is not found in the Dīghanikāya and in the Saṁyuttanikāya (Schmithausen 1981 p. 216 note 55); this may be interpreted as a rejection of the claim related to this formula by the groups who looked after these Nikāyas.

planation, but the structure of the text indicates a later addition of this judgement.[12] It appears that the old opinion was that one anticipated nirvana in the state of cessation (and it is not possible to judge nirvana as arising or passing away). One can also find this interpretation in the Visuddhimagga. But here this anticipation of nirvana is no longer a means of becoming released from rebirth; it is more a symptom of having reached this release through discriminating insight or almost having reached it.

---

[12] See Schmithausen 1981 p. 217 and 236.

CHAPTER THIRTEEN

# THE THREE REALMS OF EXISTENCE

A great part of Buddhist transmission reflects the firm conviction that some persons can master four stages of meditation on pure elements (and colours) and four stages beyond such pure forms and finally reach the cessation of apperceptions and feelings. But, in general, it is not considered necessary to utilize this possibility; salvation through discriminating insight (which in some way or other may be meditatively prepared) is sufficient. However the conviction that some persons can obtain states associated with pure forms and formlessness did leave its mark on a division of the world in three realms or layers of existence. Though sometimes implied by statements, in the Suttapiṭaka this tripartition can be found as such only at a few places (e.g. MN III p.63, DN III p.215, 275):

1. the realm of objects of desire (*kāma-dhātu*)
2. the realm of visible forms [not eliciting desire] (*rūpa-dhātu*)
3. the realm devoid of visible forms (*arūpa-dhātu*).

In later times this division was widely accepted and explained as follows. The realm of visible forms not eliciting desire consists of four strata which correspond to four stages of dhyāna[1]. The realm devoid of visible forms (in Sanskrit mostly *ārūpyadhātu*) also consists of four strata which correspond to meditation on the four spheres. In this way we arrive at nine strata (*kāmadhātu* plus 4 strata *rūpadhātu* plus 4 strata *arūpdhātu*) which, in certain considerations, are utilized[2].

Depending on the degree of spiritual development one can be reborn in any one of these realms and strata.[3] In three of the strata belonging to the realm devoid of visible forms we may discern a re-externalization

---

[1] The term *rūpa-dhātu* points to particular ideas concerning the way in which dhyāna via concentration on elements and colours originates (see chapter 12). There is no indication of these ideas in the passages on dhyāna-meditation used in chapter 1.

[2] E.g. in the description of the path to salvation in Abhidharmakośa VI. Note that in cosmography the strata of the realm which is devoid of visible forms do not lie above the strata of the realm of visible forms. A person who is destined for the realm devoid of forms enters one of its four strata at the same place where he has died (Abhidharmakośabhāṣya III 3, p. 112,6). Here, the highest place of the world is the fourth stratum of the realm of visible forms, more precisely, the highest place in this stratum, the abode of the Akaniṣṭha gods (ibid. III 2, p. 111,23).

[3] For more information see Abhidharmakośa III 1-3. Cf. Lamotte, Histoire p.34-35 and Takasaki Jikido, An Introduction to Buddhism, Tokyo 1987, 133-136.

of areas which originally were probably thought of as being external, be it in another manner, i.e., in the sphere of the infinity of space, the sphere of the infinity of perception and the sphere of nothingness (see chapter 12). Probably only a psychic "sphere" was meant by the phrase "neither apperception nor nonapperception". This now also became a stratum of the world; it was called the most superior [stratum] of [changing] existence (P. *bhavagga*, S. *bhavāgra*).

Above the most superior stratum of the world there lies, metaphorically, another sphere, the cessation of all suffering, which surpasses all realms and strata. In Udāna 8,1 the aim of religious aspiration is defined in this way. This can be deduced from the negation of the four elements, (which can be interpreted as the layer of visible forms not eliciting desire) and of the four spheres (the infinity of space, etc.,). This highest "sphere" is a kind of externalization of a "psychic state" that is beyond all states. Udāna 8,1 states, "Monks, there is a sphere where earth [does] not [exist], nor water, nor fire, nor air, nor the sphere of the infinity of space, nor the sphere of the infinity of perception, nor the sphere of nothingness, nor the sphere of neither apperception nor nonapperception, neither this world nor the world hereafter, neither the moon nor the sun. Monks, this I call not coming, not leaving, not standing, not disappearing, not appearing [again], this (I call) without foundation, without movement, without support; this is the end of suffering.

# IV. KARMA

CHAPTER FOURTEEN

# KARMA IN ANCIENT TIMES

The Sanskrit word *karma* (P. *kamma*) means "deed". In a religious context it mostly refers to an action which has, apart from an immediately visible consequence, a result after some time, generally after death. Often also the latent energy is meant which is left behind by such a deed and later produces the result. Even for that result the word *karma* is sometimes employed.

In this chapter I want to describe the ideas about karma as they were probably adopted and enriched by the Buddha and his first disciples. This will first be done by contrasting ancient Buddhism with the opinion of Ajita Kesakambala and the oldest Vedic sources on rebirth and thereby establishing that according to ancient Buddhism good deeds lead to heaven and bad deeds to the underworld. Then some reasons will be given why the Buddha, though believing that good deeds lead to heaven, strove for salvation from rebirth. In this connection the sutta on light and darkness will be cited. That good and bad deeds originally were only connected with heaven and the underworld can also be shown by the well-known formula of the divine eye. Then the distinction between intention and deed will be discussed, and also the principle by which deeds are determined as good or bad and the main rules for the laity which are derived from this principle; this will be illustrated by examples of deeds which lead to heaven or to the underworld or—what cannot be found in the oldest documents, but seems soon to be introduced, probably by the Buddha himself—to a good or bad situation in the human world.

Until now there was no reason for giving greater attention to karma, because it is not mentioned in the schemes of salvation discussed in the previous chapters. These schemes did not recognize karma as *the* or *a* cause of being reborn. In chapter 10 I have discussed and rejected the possibility that originally karma was meant by the terms *saṅkhārā* and/or *bhavo* in the twelvefold chain of dependent origination.

One can however be fairly certain that the Buddha believed that, if one was not released, good deeds would result after death in a good consequence, and bad deeds in a bad consequence. This can be deduced from an old explanation of the first requirement in the noble eightfold path which was mentioned in Chapter 3 (note 3): "He has the right views, ...: that which is given exists, that which is sacrificed exists, that which is poured [into the sacred fire] exists, the fruit, i.e. retribution, of good and evil actions exists, the world here exists, the other world exists, the mother exists, the father exists, beings who appear [spontaneously in heaven or in the underworld] exist, in the world ascetics and Brahmans exist who have gone and followed the right path and who [correctly] describe this world and the other world from their own experience and realization."

This explanation is a defence against the denial of invisible consequences of ritual and (im-)moral deeds. Very likely it is only an inversion of (a portion of) the teaching of Ajita Kesakambala, a philosopher of the time (cf. DN 2, I p.55). By this inversion ancient Buddhism formed a common front with the Brahmans against all philosophers who denied the other world ( = the world hereafter) and not directly visible consequences of ritual and (im-)moral deeds. This explanation and the opinion of Ajita, of which it seems to be an inversion, contain rather archaic formulations. It is probable that the Buddha already at the beginning of his career faced such a denial of karma. What he and his followers said about the consequences of our deeds would therefore be a conscious choice and not a naive conviction.

The most ancient places found in the Vedas where rebirth is mentioned show only a belief in the other world, not in consequences of our deeds. After a stay in heaven a person is reborn as a human being, preferably in his own family; birds were also considered a stage in the transition from one existence to the other.[1] From this we may deduce that in India the doctrine of rebirth was not a corollary of the desire for justice, as it perhaps was in late Judaism. But such a desire for justice and the belief—often not in agreement with such a desire—that the power of rites goes beyond this life soon led to the conviction that only the person who has invested in good deeds or special rites goes to heaven after death; other persons go to the underworld. This seems to be the situation the Buddha found and accepted at the beginning of his career. Rites have however no place in the ancient teaching and are severely rejected when they are supposed to supersede immoral actions. Soon also the idea was introduced that good or bad deeds need not always lead to heaven or the underworld, but can be requited in the next human existence (and, later, in the realms of animals and hungry ghosts).

Against the latter view the old Vedic position perhaps was defended by some persons. In the Milindapañha (p.5) it is told that Makkhali Gosāla

[1] See M. Witzel, The oldest form of the idea of rebirth. Lecture, 32. CISHAAN, Tokyo-Kyoto, 1983.

had the following opinion: a warrior again becomes a warrior, a Brahman again becomes a Brahman, a Caṇḍāla again becomes a Caṇḍāla; there is no ripening of good and bad deeds in a future (human) existence. Makkhali is known from other sources, e.g. DN I p.53-54, as an older contemporary of the Buddha. He is said to have proclaimed that everyone has to undergo countless rebirths and that after aeons everyone is released without regard to his intellectual and moral state. He denied any effect of human deeds, especially in respect to salvation.

If the Buddha was convinced that one's deeds and probably (as we see in MN 136) also one's convictions in the hour of death regulate what happens after death, one could wonder why he did strive for release from rebirth instead of a long sojourn in heaven, using a new human existence after this to again strive for heaven. But it seems clear that he was as much displeased with the transientness of these visits in heaven, even if they were relatively long, as he was frightened by the prospect of a new human existence which, even under the best circumstances, is always accompanied by old age and death. Moreover, it is difficult to see how a material existence can totally avoid living at the cost of other living creatures. As we will see below, the primary criterion for good and bad is the avoidance and non-avoidance of doing harm to others. The retribution of minor bad deeds can be postponed, but not indefinitely, because they will accumulate (the idea that bad deeds can be compensated by meritorious deeds apparently was not yet known or accepted). Therefore one has also to undergo a sojourn in the underworld at some time, which is worse than a human existence (though in the first period it was not yet conceived of as a hell[2]). Finally, he had to strive for salvation, because (as we will see below) in that time people were not considered sure of their knowledge of good and evil and their character in a future human life, and therefore bad behavior which is more than only trying to survive could not be excluded, and this leads soon or directly to the underworld.

That one cannot be sure of one's behavior in a future existence can be demonstrated with SN 3.21, the sutta on light and darkness. It still reflects the old structure that good or bad conduct in the world of mankind leads either to heaven or to the underworld.

The following is a brief summary of the contents of this sutta. There are four kinds of persons (*puggala*); one who from the darkness goes to

---

[2] The result after death of bad deeds is generally indicated by the following clause (e.g. MN 136, III p.209): *apāyaṁ duggatiṁ vinipātaṁ nirayaṁ uppajjati*. Not all of these quasi synonyms do have to go back to the most ancient times. The last one means "hell". A difference between *vinipāta* and *niraya* can still be found in MN 12 (I p.73): *katamā ... opapātikā yoni: devā nerayikā ekacce ca manussā ekacce ca vinipātikā ...*

the darkness, one who from the darkness goes to the light, one who from the light goes to the darkness, and one who from the light goes to the light. The person who from the darkness goes to the darkness is reborn (*paccājāto*) in a lower class family of Caṇḍālas, basketmakers, hunters, etc., in a poor family with little food and clothing; moreover the person is ugly and a cripple. And this person leads an evil life with his body, his speech and his thoughts and after death he goes to the underworld. The person who from the darkness goes to the light is also reborn in a lower class family of Caṇḍālas, etc., is ugly and a cripple, but leads a good life with his body, his speech, and his thoughts and after death goes to the heavenly world. The person who from the light goes to the darkness is reborn in a upper class family of wealthy warriors, Brahmans, or citizens where there are all the luxuries of life; moreover the person is beautiful. This person leads an evil life with his body, his speech and his thoughts, and after death he goes to the underworld. Finally, the person who from the light goes to the light is reborn in a upper class family of wealthy warriors, Brahmans or citizens where there are all the luxuries of life; moreover the person is beautiful. This person leads a good life with his body, his speech, and his thoughts and after death he goes to the heavenly world.

According to this sutta neither the social environment nor a beautiful or ugly body determine how one will think and act. Neither is this determined by previous thoughts and acts, if we, according to later developments, assume that karma also is the cause of a birth in a high or low class family etc.. We will see in chapter 15 that changes do occur in respect to this concept.

The idea that nothing is determined in the future may have been one of the Buddha's motives to strive for salvation. But he also seems to have been clear that many persons were impressed neither by this nor by other motives. I see no problem in ascribing to him quite a few instructions to lay people for reaching heaven and avoiding the underworld, and, after some time, for improving the circumstances of a future human life. A prosperous human life can also be seen as better grounds for the path to salvation than poverty where people are absorbed by the worries of daily life and are more reluctant to give up their property than the sons (later also: the daughters) of rich families. This idea, which reflects the fact that most members of the Buddhist order came from upper class families, is illustrated in MN 66 by the parable of the elephant which tears a strong fetter and the quail which cannot release itself from a rotten cord.

Passages in the canon which mention the "divine eye" are also grounds for assuming that in the earliest period the idea of karma was only connected with heaven and the underworld and not with a future human existence. If we look at MN 136, the divine eye does not appear as the Buddha's discovery and a faculty only known to Buddhists. The formula of the divine eye in the detailed dhyāna path, which can not be accepted as belonging to the original enlightenment of the Buddha[3], reflects the same ancient ideas about karma.

In MN 136 (III p. 210) we find the following passage: An ascetic or a brahman, who exerts himself to the greatest degree, achieves such a concentration of the mind (*cetosamādhi*), that he can see with the divine eye (*dibbena cakkhunā*) how a person, who has brought harm to another (and trespassed other principal rules of asceticism), goes to the underworld. But another ascetic sees with the divine eye how someone, who

[3] The main philological argument is that in MN 112 (III p. 33-36) the detailed description of the dhyāna path is cast in the form of a monk's report of the attainment of salvation. The end of this report also appears in MN 4 (I p. 21) and in MN 36 (I p.247), but here it is a report made by the Buddha. MN 112 does not contain the knowledge of one's former existences and of the disappearance and reappearance of other creatures. MN 4 and 36 do include these two types of knowledge, but are, in this passage, divergent from the other report in that the usual aorist tense is replaced by the present tense. This makes it clear that here we are dealing with formulas which were derived from other traditions and which already had a fixed form. Consequently it appears that MN 112 contains an older form of the report. But the report in MN 112 seems to have come forth from a period in which, generally, others have taken over from the Buddha the task of preaching. The rather ancient—in relation to the concluding parts—beginning of this detailed description is adapted in that one could also hear the doctrine from a disciple of the Tathāgata (III p. 33,6) and thereby gain trust in the Tathāgata and abandon the life of the householder. However, in the suttas MN 4 and MN 36 we find apparently very ancient "I"-reports in the aorist tense of Gotama's striving for salvation. Consequently it is not surprising that later, when it was felt necessary, these suttas were extended with an I-report on a formulated liberating insight and that the end of the I-report in MN 112, which was also written in the aorist tense, was chosen. But this I-report is no longer that of an ordinary monk, it is now the Buddha's. The salvation of the Buddha must also be his enlightenment. In the course of time everything that an author considered essential for Buddhism had to be thought of as having been revealed at the moment of enlightenment, or in the days afterward. The remembrance of one's former existences and the observation of the disappearance and reappearance of other creatures belonged now to these essentials. The first became the Buddhist basis for the belief in rebirth and the second for the belief in the retaliation for one's deeds. For this aim formulas were used here which already existed (perhaps before the Buddha). From this starting-point the remembrance of one's rebirths and the observation of the disappearance and reappearance of other creatures may have been adopted in the detailed description of the dhyāna path in other suttas. Cf. Schmithausen 1981, 221 note 75 (referring also to Bareau *Recherches* pp. 81 ff.)

One could surmise that the observation of the disappearance and reappearance of other creatures does not lead to the realization of the four noble truths on its own accord because non-Buddhists are also said to have it, at least to a lesser degree, as we have seen in MN 136. But it could still be a good preparation for this realization. This is different from the remembrance of one's former existences, which, according to the Brahmajālasutta (DN I p. 13), can be the origin of the opinion that the self and the world are eternal.

has brought harm to others, goes to the heavenly world. Yet another ascetic sees with the divine eye how a person who has brought no harm to others, goes to the heavenly world. And yet another ascetic sees with the divine eye how someone, who has brought no harm to others, goes to the underworld.

All these ascetics are accused of generalizing too quickly on their limited observations. If, for example, someone, who has brought harm to others, is found in the heavenly world, then that does not mean that bad deeds are not requited, but that this person had accumulated a supply of good deeds which carried more weight than the more recent evil deeds, or that the person had the right views at the hour of death. The Buddha, who is the authority quoted as having made these censorious remarks, apparently sees further with his divine eye in space and time than the other ascetics and, moreover, he combines the data better.

The divine eye is identical to the second of the two types of knowledge which in the detailed description of the dhyāna path have been inserted between the attainment of the fourth stage of dhyāna and the realization of the four noble truths. This second type of knowledge is described (cf. e.g. MN 27, I p.183) as follows (abridged):

> ''With (his) divine eye he sees creatures disappearing and reappearing, the lowly and the exalted, beautiful and ugly, with a blessed existence or a miserable existence. He understands that they return in accordance with their deeds. Some creatures do evil with their body, their speech and their thoughts. They condemn the noble (*ariya*), they have wrong views and conduct themselves [conformable to these] wrong views; after death they reappear in the underworld. But other creatures do good with their body, their speech and their thoughts. They do not condemn the noble, they have the right views and conduct themselves [conformable to these] right views; after death they reappear in the heavenly world.''

The theoreticians of the dhyāna path thought that also a remembrance of one's former existences belonged to the enlightenment and release of the Buddha and his better disciples[4]. But the formula of the remem-

[4] These disciples are called *tevijja* (possessing the threefold knowledge, the third knowledge being liberating insight into the four noble truths plus destruction of the cankers. In SN 8.7 we find an interesting division of Arhats. The greater part of 500 Arhats is said to have been released by discriminating insight, but sixty possess the threefold knowledge, sixty possess supernatural power (*abhiññā*, i.e., the threefold knowledge, miraculous power, being able to hear divine sounds and to penetrate the heart of another), and sixty have been ''released from both parts'' (cf. Edgerton BHSD s.v. *ubhayato-bhāga-vimukta*), i.e., have been emancipated from the cankers (by discriminating insight?) *and* are able to reach the cessation of apperceptions and feelings (*saññā-vedayita-nirodha*) in which they are freed from all suffering here and now. Cf. P. Demiéville, Sur la mémoire des existences antérieures. *Bulletin de l'Ecole française d'Extrême Orient* 27 (1927) p. 286. The supernatural powers are missing in the Chinese versions. Ninety monks possess the threefold knowledge and ninety monks fall under the last

brance of former existences, which is perhaps also very old but comes from a different source, does not mention a heaven and an underworld, nor karmic retribution, it is only concerned with rebirth in the world of man. It states (e.g. in MN I p.22, abridged):

> "I remember one former existence, two, three,...ten, twenty, thirty,...a hundred, a thousand, a hundred thousand, numerous aeons in which the world approaches destruction, numerous aeons in which the world expands... There I had this name, belonged to this family, this caste, had this livelihood, experienced this happiness and sorrow, lived so long; having disappeared from there I reappeared here, had this name...".

The juxtaposition of the two formulas allowed persons to mentally combine them and read in them what they expected to find there, namely that the quality of human existence is also the effect of karma.

At one place in the Pāli canon, at the beginning of MN 130, we find a description of the divine eye which is adapted in such a way that persons who do good with their body, their speech and their thought not only reappear in heaven, but also among mankind, and persons who do evil with their body, their speech and their thought not only reappear in the underworld (which is now a real hell with several departments, supervised by king Yama), but also in the realms of the hungry ghosts (originally the dead immediately after death and a stage for all persons[5]) or the animals. It is not easy to ascribe this sutta to the Buddha and his first disciples. The destiny of mankind is quite superficially seen as the result of good deeds without any attention to miserable situations. And a hell is pictured in too glaring colours. But some developments may be expected within the long lifetime of the Buddha, especially that differences in human existence are explained by karma (not in this sutta) and that after death one does not always go to heaven or the underworld, but that one becomes directly a human being if one has no extremely good or bad karma. Heaven[6] and underworld are no longer transit stages to a new

---

category, released from both parts. In this way we again arrive at a number of 180 monks who have not been released merely through discriminating insight.

[5] The polemic sutta AN 10.17.11 is interesting in this context. In it the Buddha is reported to say to the brahman Janussoni: You can go on with making offerings to dead members of the family. It is true that many will not profit from this because they have been reborn somewhere else, but there is certainly always someone in the family who finds himself amongst the hungry ghosts. Moreover you, at any rate, profit by making offerings because gifts to the dead are also deserving.
In later times a similar idea comes back into Buddhism. Some schools (cf. Bareau, Les Sectes p.291) entertain the concept of an intermediary stage (*antarābhava*, in Tibetan: *bardo*) of some weeks immediately after death and before entering a new existence (Cf. Abhidharmakośa III 4-14).

[6] In this time the belief in more than one heaven must be assumed. To mention a few, one may be reborn in the heaven of the 33 gods led by Indra (see chapter 15). Even higher

human existence, but places of rebirth just as the world of mankind, of animals and of hungry ghosts.

We now come to the question by what principle are deeds called good or bad in the time of the Buddha and his first disciples. First and foremost we must establish that by karma is meant deeds by body, speech and thought, as can be gathered from all citations in this chapter. It is not only a deed by the body as the word *karma* might suggest, nor is it only a deed by thought or an intention, as one might expect from later developments supported by a few passages in the canon (e.g. AN 6.6.9, see chapter 10).

In ancient times the most important characteristic which makes deeds good or bad is that they have to do with the well-being of others in a positive or negative sense. In this respect one can distinguish a) to do good to another living being or leave it undone, though it would be possible and necessary, and b) to avoid injuring another living being, though this would be possible and seemingly necessary, or fail to avoid injuring.

In the inversion of Ajita Kesakambala's opinion cited above we find also the possibility of ritual karma which as such and without special objectives does not serve the well-being of other living beings, or does serve the well-being of some creatures at the expense of others. Ancient Buddhism did not need this possibility. However, after the death of the Buddha many Buddhists considered the worship of a stupa containing (or supposed to contain) a relic of the master or of one of his disciples or (mythical) predecessors a means of acquiring good karma and not only a means of purifying the mind. This kind of karma could perhaps be brought under the heading of ritual karma. Later, in Tantrism, we can find rites in the full sense of the word.

---

is the Tusita heaven, where, according to a later opinion, every future Buddha stays before he attains enlightenment here on earth (see chapter 15); the highest is the Brahma heaven. When the world was divided into three layers (see chapter 13), all these heavens, with the exception of the Brahma heaven, were relegated to the layer of the objects of desire (*kāmadhātu*). These heavens are now the upper story of the layer of the objects of desire, underneath is the world of man, the kingdom of the hungry ghosts, the animal kingdom and lastly the hells. The Brahma world became the lowest point in the layer of visible forms [not eliciting desire] (*rūpa-dhātu*).

Having command of higher meditative states determines rebirth in the layer of forms and the layer devoid of visible forms (see chapter 13). This mastery, in order to incorporate it into the terminology of a doctrine of karma which regulates all kinds of rebirth, was later called "immovable" (S. *aniñjya*) karma. It is a third kind of karma along with goed (S. *kuśala*) karma and harmful (S. *akuśala*) karma. See Edgerton BHSD s.v. *aniñjya*; see also Abhidharmakośa IV 45-46. However in the Visuddhimagga (ed. Warren/Kosambi p. 451, 465 and 476) *āneñjābhisaṅkhāra* seems to refer to the layer devoid of forms only.

As to the above-mentioned criterion of the well-being of other living beings and the distiction between a) actively doing some good to others or not, and b) refraining from injuring others or not, the following illustration can be given for a):

The notion of liberality (*dāna*) will have been the focal point in this teaching. One must see this concept in the context of giving support to the Buddhist order. But it seems that less emphasis was laid on this point in the beginning (in the sutta cited at the end of this chapter one has to give to "ascetics and Brahmans"), than in later times. Furthermore (in, for example, SN 7.19, Sn v.98) caring for one's parents is mentioned, and (in SN 1.47) planting parks, building bridges, digging wells, and giving shelter to the homeless[7]. The value of a deed is not only determined by the deed itself. In SN 1.32 it is stated that giving from poverty is worth more than a gift easily missed. This concept links up quite well with the attitude of self denial which is so characteristic of the most ancient path to salvation.

With b) is meant that the laity should follow the ascetic rules[8] for the preparation of dhyāna (see chapter 6) as much as is possible in the life of a householder. In this way laypersons could do good deeds and especially avoid evil deeds, which was probably the oldest (non-Buddhist) purpose behind these rules. Of course this also means some preparation for dhyāna, and on Buddhist "Sundays" the laity can try to strictly imitate monks and nuns. In Sn 400-404 one can find an outline of the prescriptions for these days; there it is said that by keeping to these special rules a layperson goes, after death, to the gods "which are radiating light from themselves" (*sayampabha*).

To illustrate most of the rules for everyday life and their connection with expectations of the future consequences of our deeds I will now present a passage from MN 135, a sutta which also documents the new development that situations in human life are explained by the karma of a former life.

Such an explanation may even be the main aim of the sutta. It begins with the question, how can it be that some people experience bad times and other people good times. Some have a long life, others a short one; somc arc oftcn ill, others hardly ever; some are beautiful, others ugly; some enjoy great power, others hardly any; some belong to lower class

---

[7] More details may be found in DN 31 (cf. Sn 91-142, 258-269).

[8] Later reduced to five regulations, refraining from killing, stealing, illegitimate sexual activity, lying and (cf. Sn 264) the carelessness caused by strong liquor and the like (e.g. DN 5 I p. 146).

families, others to upper class families; some have hardly any intellect, others a great deal. The answer is that all is the consequence of deeds, the creatures are the inheritors of their deeds (*kammadayāda*).

Then there is a discussion of the differences mentioned. If a woman or a man kills living creatures and shows no mercy to them, then she or he will go to the underworld after death, or, if that is not the case, she or he will not enjoy a long life amongst mankind. But if a woman or a man refrains from killing, touches no weapon, is full of compassion, then she or he will go to the heavenly world, or, if that is not the case, she or he will enjoy a long life amongst mankind.

The remaining points are discussed in the same manner. If we now restrict ourselves to the world of man, we find the following description. Whoever injures another will often be ill; whoever does not do this will hardly ever be ill. Whoever is irascible will be ugly; whoever is well-disposed will be good-looking. Whoever is jealous and begrudges the property and honour of others will later on have little or no power or influence; whoever does not do this will later on have great power and influence. Whoever does not give food, clothing, etc., to ascetics and Brahmans will later on have little property; whoever does this will later on possess much property. Whoever is proud and does not pay homage to those who deserve honour will later on be reborn in a lower class family; whoever is not proud and pays homage to those who deserve honour will later on be reborn in an upper class family. Whoever does not approach ascetics and Brahmans and does not ask what is detrimental and what is beneficial will later on have little intellect; whoever does this will later on possess great intellect.

CHAPTER FIFTEEN

# LATER DEVELOPMENTS

This last chapter will deal with later developments in thought on karma. Not everything that will be mentioned has been accepted everywhere in Buddhism.

Probably in the first centuries after the Buddha's death the following ideas were introduced or became important:

1. all evil deeds must be requited or at least be superseded by good deeds before a person can become released,
2. pleasant and unpleasant feelings in a human existence are the result of former deeds,
3. evil behavior and its results form a vicious circle from which one can hardly escape,
4. Gotama could become Buddha because he did good deeds through countless former lives, devoting their result to the aim of enlightenment,
5. by confession and repentance one can (partly) annul an evil deed,
6. evil deeds of non-Arhats (as to Arhats see point 1) can be superseded by great merits,
7. one can and should transfer merit to others, especially for their spiritual development.

Not all of these ideas seem to be capable of existing harmoniously together. But at some places and times many of them really did so. The best explanation may be that Buddhism underwent a growing influence of retribution thinking (in early times mainly represented by Jainism), but at the same time it developed defence mechanisms.

I only want to mention, but not discuss the points 5), 6) and 7). They are best documented by noncanonical sources, which testify to their great importance in everyday religious life.[1]

---

[1] Confession and repentance of bad deeds seem to be an old means of spiritual guidance, "for he who acknowledges his transgression and confesses it for betterment in future, will grow in the Ariyan discipline" (as M. Walshe, *Thus Have I Heard* London 1987 p.108, translates the relevant passage at the end of DN 2). But that thereby the future consequences of evil deeds can be diminished or eliminated is probably a new development. At the end of DN 2 king Ajātaśatru confesses and repents having murdered his father. In the Pāli-version (I p.85) this seems to have no effect on the karma already done (cf. R.O. Franke, *Dīghanikāya*, Göttingen 1913, p.84 note 5). But one of the Chinese parallel versions presented by K. Meisig in *Das Śrāmaṇyaphala-Sūtra* (Wiesbaden 1987, 365) has this idea.

The other items are arranged in such a way that the one with the greatest consequence for the history of ideas, namely that Gotama became a Buddha by his aspiration and deeds in former lives, is discussed last. It is the starting-point of the main aim of the Great Vehicle (*mahāyāna*), that as many persons as possible should themselves become a Buddha. At this point we definitively leave the theme of ideas and meditative practices of *Early* Buddhism.

### 1. *Retribution of all deeds*

We may assume that the Buddha did not consider it necessary that karma should have been entirely requited before a person could become released. Good karma does not make a person an Arhat and bad karma cannot prevent a person from abstaining from evil conduct and following a path to salvation and eventually becoming an Arhat. After the death of an Arhat there is no possibility of retribution in heaven or in the underworld, nor in another destiny. But after a while the idea emerges that the karma of this life can already be requited in this same life.[2] This seems to be due to the demand that the evil deeds done by an Arhat before entering religious life also must be requited. Note that not even the relatively late idea of the five bad deeds[3] unworthy of respite (S. *ānantarya-karma*) and leading directly to hell after death is originally conceived in such a way that this karma directly causes death or has other consequences in this life, though some later legends report that a sinner was swallowed up by the fires of the lowest hell immediately after his (or her) deed.

---

As to the supersession of evil karma of non-Arhats by great merits see R. Gombrich, *Precept and Practice*, Oxford 1971, 215-216. The only specific case heard of in Ceylon seems to be king Duṭṭhagāmanī (101-77 B.C.). He killed many Tamils in war, but he did it to save Buddhism. His merits (also by founding monasteries, etc.) so far outweighed his bad karma that he will stay in heaven till the time of Maitrī, the next Buddha, when he will be reborn as his right-hand disciple and attain nirvana.

A lucid exposition of the complex matter that is called merit transference in modern Ceylon and of some canonical passages which show a beginning of this practice is given by R. Gombrich in the book just mentioned, pp. 226-243. Literature on merit transference in Ceylon is gathered by J. W. de Jong in *Indo Iranian Journal* 1982, 313 (note 1). For other regions and aspects see G. Schopen, Two Problems in the History of Indian Buddhism: The Layman/Monk Distinction and the Doctrines of the Transference of Merit, *Studien zur Indologie und Iranistik*, Heft 10, 1984, 9-47.

[2] This can be found in the same passage of AN 6.6.9 (III p.415) which tries to reduce karma to intention (*cetanā*). There are three kinds of retribution of karma, already in this life, in the next existence, or after the next existence.

[3] E.g. Vibhaṅga Nal. ed. p 454 and Abhidharmakośa III 96105: causing a schism (*saṅghabheda*), matricide, patricide, killing an Arhat and wounding a Tathāgata (who cannot be killed). Devadatta is said to have caused a schism and injured the Buddha.

To illustrate this point I shall review two canonical reports on Aṅgulimāla. According to the nucleus of these reports Aṅgulimāla was a robber and murderer who, after an encounter with the Buddha, became a monk and shortly after attained Arhatship. Since he had become a monk and the Buddha had answered for him, he was not persecuted by the king.

The perhaps oldest report in the Pāli canon, Theragāthā 866-891, points to the problem of the former evil deeds of Aṅgulimāla in two verses. In v.872 we read that a person whose former evil deeds are covered by good deeds illuminates this world like the moon which is no longer behind the clouds. And in v.882 Aṅgulimāla says that after having done deeds which normally lead to the underworld he has now been touched by the retribution of karma and is eating his food without guilt. The context hardly contributes to the understanding of these verses. The first one could be interpreted as an allusion to the supersession of bad karma by good karma. But it is also possible that it only means that Aṅgulimāla as an Arhat causes us to forget that he was a robber and murderer. The second verse speaks of retribution, but we cannot see of what kind.

The second report, MN 86, is made up of prose and verses; the verses are the same as Theragāthā 866-886. Two passages of the prose portion deal with our problem and can perhaps be employed as a commentary to the above mentioned verses. The monk Aṅgulimāla, when he was not yet an Arhat, is reported (MN II p.103) to have helped a woman who was having difficulties in giving birth to her child by pronouncing the following words: I am not aware of having consciously taken life since I was born in the noble birth; may you and your child be well by means of this truth (*tena saccena*). The second passage (MN II p.104) reports that Aṅgulimāla, after having reached Arhatship, once while begging has all kinds of things thrown at him and becomes injured. The Buddha is said to have comforted him by interpreting this as a substitution for thousands of years of punishment in hell (*niraya*, indicating a real hell).[4]

That he had assisted the woman and her child and that he had not consciously taken life since he was spiritually reborn (which latter fact, pronounced as a truth, was used as a remedy) could be seen as the good karma by which (portions of) his former evil deeds have been superseded. However the second passage does not allude to such a supersession. It seems only to assume a requital of bad karma by experiencing its results,

[4] Research carried out by A. Bareau (Annuaire du College de France 1985-1986, Resumé des cours et travaux, p. 654-658) establishes the fact that the oldest transmission of the story does not contain this episode.

though what is described there does not amount to much. We can imagine that the Buddha comforted Aṅgulimāla by saying: when you have such experiences you must think of all the injuries you yourself inflicted upon others. But the formulation we now have before us is an attempt to show that the principle of retaliation of all evil deeds is also valid in the case of an Arhat.

The principle that vaguely appeared here has been stated in clear, but abstract terms at another place. In the beginning of AN 10.21.7( + 8) it is stated that one cannot put an end to one's suffering as long as one has not destroyed the deeds which one intended to do, had really done and which were accumulated (from former existences) by having experienced their consequences here or in a later existence. The remainder of the sutta reveals that both bad and good deeds are meant. This is an opinion that in ancient times generally was ascribed to Jainism (cf. MN 101; note however that in another sutta against Jainism, MN 14, only evil deeds are mentioned). In fact it is asserted here that karma is a cause for being reborn and that one must abstain from all deeds and speed up the requital of former deeds if one wants to be released from rebirth. That this leads to absurd consequences is shown in MN 101.

In the immediate proximity of this passage, in AN 10.21.9, we find an attempt to react to this idea, which in AN 10.21.7( + 8) is presented as the Buddha's word, without directly attacking it. What is asserted in the beginning of AN 10.21.7( + 8) is accepted, but cultivating the four immeasurables (see chapter 7) is recommended as a means to overcome the power of former deeds. It is said that in these meditations no limited deed remains.[5] The sutta obviously falls back on the ancient function of these meditations. Having reached perfection in them meant that one felt

[5] The sutta then deviates from the subject in an attempt to explain what was first said. This is probably not by the same author. Deeds are now confined to bad deeds: whoever practices the states of friendliness, etc., from his earliest childhood onwards can no longer commit bad deeds. But nothing is mentioned about getting rid of the bad (and good) deeds already done.

In the texts generally nothing is said about the necessity of a retribution for *good* deeds. If one wants to have a theory in this matter, one could say: in as much as good deeds are mostly defined negatively and in conjunction with the rules of ascetism preparing for meditation, their result can be included in the result of being released. In this respect a temporary and an infinite well-being cannot strictly be divided.

In MN 57, AN 4.24.2 and DN (Saṅgīti sutta) III p. 230 we find the idea that all ( = black, white and mixed [cf. Yogasūtra IV 7]) karma must be overcome, which probably implies that here karma is accepted as a cause of rebirth. As a means to overcome all karma a "deed" (*kamma*) consisting in the intention (*cetanā*) to give up all karma is recommended. Cf. the discussion of these passages by L. Schmithausen in *Karma and Rebirth* ed. by R. W. Neufeldt, State University of New York Press, 1986, chapter 12, Critical Response p. 207.

released and did not care about the retribution of bad or good karma.[6]

The reaction described in AN 10.21.9 signals a compromise which is characteristic for further developments in this matter. Nearly all Buddhist schools accept karma as a cause of rebirth (and not only as a cause of the quality of a new existence). But this has not the practical consequence of avoiding actions and speeding up retribution which in AN 10.21.7( + 8) seem so difficult to avoid. The general solution is rather theoretical. Karma is not the sole cause of a rebirth, it needs other causes, which are called *kleśa*, such as ignorance and craving, to be able to bring forth a new existence.[7] A person who has overcome these causes by following a method of salvation need not fight his karma.

### *2. All feelings should be referred to karma*

In chapter 14 it has been shown that originally heaven and the underworld were the places for retribution of good and evil karma. At the end of that chapter MN 135 was presented where also the human world is a place of retribution and the following consequences of karma are mentioned: short or long life, often or hardly ever being ill, ugliness or beauty, little or great power, little or much property, birth in a lower or in a upper class family, little or great intellect. Pleasant and unpleasant feelings in the human world do not appear here or merely in so far as some of the situations mentioned are better suited for pleasant or unpleasant feelings than others.

Very likely it is not through negligence that feelings are not mentioned. That all feelings are a consequence of former deeds is in MN 101[8] presented as a doctrine of Jainism. We also find suttas which mention eight different causes resulting in disease (and in the pain connected with a disease) entirely of themselves without the help of the other causes. In AN 4.9.7, 5.11.4 and 10.6.10 bile, phlegm, wind, a mixture of the three, unexpected weather, an irregular lifestyle, injury and karma are enumerated. The Sīvaka sutta (SN 36.21) contains the same series and explicitly attacks any notion that one can explain everything by karma; it appeals to everyone's own experience and to generally accepted ideas.

---

[6] See also H. Beckh, *Buddhismus*, 2. Band, Berlin (2nd ed.) 1920, p. 132-135. It is stated in AN 3.10.9 that the deeds no longer have any hold on someone who practises ascetism, meditation, discriminating insight and the immeasurables (the latter are indicated by: *aparitto mahatto appamāṇavihārī*); a piece of salt when thrown into a cup of water can be tasted, but not when thrown into a river.

[7] The starting-point of this theory is perhaps the idea of the Śālistambasūtra that causes and conditions must be complete in order to produce a result. See E. Frauwallner, *Die Philosophie des Buddhismus*, Berlin, 2nd ed. 1958, 49-60.

[8] II p. 101: *Yaṁ kiñcāyaṁ purisapuggalo paṭisaṁvedeti, sukhaṁ vā dukkhaṁ vā adukkhamasukhaṁ vā, sabban taṁ pubbekatahetu.*

The notion found in MN 135 that one is frequently ill as a result of former deeds could be put under the heading of the eighth cause, karma. But the series of eight causes suggests that one only should use this explanation when all others have failed.

The Sīvaka sutta can be seen as a reaction to the increasing influence of Jainist karma theory. A similar reaction can be found in the Milindapañha. This text appeals to the Sīvaka sutta. The section pp. 134-138 which is concluded with this appeal probably does not belong to the oldest nucleus of the book and perhaps originated in the beginning of the Christian era. It is directed towards the tendency to reduce the causes of all diseases and pain to bad karma. This should also hold true for the Buddha. The wounds that, according to legend, were inflicted on him by Devadatta during a murder attempt and the illness reported in DN 16 should have been the consequences of bad deeds which were done before he became enlightened[9] But according to the Milindapañha Gotama could only reach enlightenment, which here is called omniscience, because he no longer had any bad karma (p.134). That is why this explanation for his wounds and his illness is unacceptable to it and why it falls back on the Sīvaka sutta, which mentions eight possible causes for illness. In the case of the Buddha his karma, as a cause, is not applicable to the vicissitudes in his life. The text does make a small concession here; wind (but not the other causes) can through karma become the cause of an illness (p.135).

According to Nyanatiloka[10] this opinion of the Milindapañha is not in concordance with the true doctrine of the Theravāda which refers all feelings to karma. He can explain the doctrine of the eight causes only in such a way that the karma mentioned in the eighth place means "only karma" and the remaining causes mean "indirect karma via these causes".[11] In view of MN 101 this karma theory could be called Jainist.

[9] See also Therāpadānam (Nal.ed. 39. 78-81) ... *tena kammavipākena Devadatto silaṁ khipi*... and Abhidharmakośabhāṣya IV 102 ... *na ca punaḥ sarveṣāṃ buddhānāṃ cakrabhedaḥ karmādhīnatvāt*.

[10] *Die Fragen des Milindo*, München-Neubiberg [1924], 216, note 121; in the edition revised by Nyanaponika (Milindapañha, Die Fragen des Königs Milinda, Interlaken 1985) this opinion remains fully accepted (p. 154, note 38).

[11] Cf. W. Halbfass, Karma, *apūrva* and "Natural" causes: Observations on the Growth and Limits of the Theory of Saṃsāra, in : *Karma and Rebirth in Classical Indian Tradition* ed. W.D. O'Flaherty, Berkely 1980, 295-296, and J.P. McDermott, Karma and Rebirth in early Buddhism, in the same book, p. 175-176. See also R.F. Gombrich, *Precept and Practice*, Oxford 1971, p.150.

We find a similar discussion in Milindapañha p. 301-309: does everyone die at the time determined by his karma? The answer is no. In A. Bareau, Der indische Buddhismus, in: *Die Religionen Indiens II*, Stuttgart 1964, 96-97, 101-102 and 105 one can get an impression as to what extent the various schools of Buddhism differed in relation to comparable problems. Unfortunately only brief statements have been transmitted.

### 3. *The vicious circle of evil deeds and bad results*

In chapter 14 the sutta of light and darkness was outlined. We got the impression that nobody is predestined to good or evil deeds by his social environment or bodily conditions. At the end of the chapter we became acquainted with the contents of MN 135. Little intelligence in a new human life appeared amongst the consequences of bad deeds. We might imagine that such a consequence leads to a behavior that again has bad results. But the text itself hardly suggests this. It rather teaches that one has to listen to ascetics and Brahmans; the result will be great intelligence in future.

Oppressive however is the vision which is propagated by MN 129, the sutta of the fool and the wise person. The original intention probably was to admonish by exaggerating the consequences if one would not listen. But this resulted in a sutta whose theoretical structure hardly seems to allow any change. People are divided into two groups in this sutta, fools and wise persons. A fool is someone who thinks evil thoughts, speaks evil words, and commits evil actions. He is already punished in this life by the opinion others have of him and a bad conscience and after death he goes to the underworld. A wise person is someone who thinks good thoughts, speaks good words, and does good actions. He is respected and has a clean conscience and after death he goes to heaven.

This is one of the first texts which have a real hell instead of an abstractly formulated underworld; it attempts to teach it by illustration (see also MN 130 which was mentioned in chapter 14, and Kokālika sutta Sn III 10). This is also one of the first texts that recognizes the kingdom of animals as a destiny after death (but not yet that of the hungry ghosts, cf. MN 57). Suffering there is said to be terrible as well. It is very difficult to become a human again once one has gone to the kingdom of animals [and to the hell(?)]. It is quicker for a tortoise, who lives in the great ocean and once in a hundred years rises out of the water, to put his head in a yoke which is blown by the wind back and forth on the water, than for a fool who has sunk to the depths to become a human again. That is because in the kingdom of animals [and also in the hell(?)] the one preys on the other; righteous living does not exist. But if a fool does succeed to become a human again after a long time, then he will become a Caṇḍāla or a member of some other low caste, he will be ugly and disabled, and he will again lead a bad life which will put him back in hell [or in the kingdom of animals(?)]. But if the wise person, after a long time, leaves heaven, then he will be reborn amongst warriors, brahmans, or citizens, will be beautiful and not disabled. He will lead a good life and go back to heaven.

The brackets I put in my summary indicate that this sutta is not so well composed as to show that the passage about rebirth amongst animals is an addition and originally perhaps an independent piece. This addition contains one of the most oppressive remarks of the whole sutta, namely that "there ( = in the realm of animals) righteous living ... meritorious action does not exist, there ... preying on each other, killing the weaker ones prevails" (*na h' ettha ... atthi dhammacariyā ... kusalakiriyā ..., aññamaññakhādikā ettha ... vattati dubbalamārikā*, III p.169). It is difficult to see how this is consonant with two remarks made earlier in the sutta (III p.167) that there are animals eating grass (*tiṇabhakkha*) and that there are animals eating excrement (*gūthabhakkha*)[12]. It is also not compatible with other Buddhist tales, probably also of that time, where animals, i.e. the Buddha in a former life, find a way to help others (see section 5 below). Attempting to read synthetically, as most Buddhists will have done, we could say: Righteous deeds in that realm are an exception. Normally an animal has few chances to do good deeds, but it often commits evil deeds. Bad karma increases through the evil deeds and prevents the residue of good karma, which most beings might possess, from enabling them to return to the human world after experiencing the consequences of their former bad deeds. That is to say, the realm of the animals, and perhaps also hell, is considered a place of retribution *and* action, not only of retribution.

One could observe that in this sutta at least nothing is said about the determination by karma of the intelligence of a person. However nothing can happen in this respect, because the fool and the wise person are the subjects of the entire story. The text does not mention a change in their situation, though its sole intention might have been that the fool becomes a wise person and the latter does not become a fool. Also note that the assertions concerning the consequences of a bad or good family or having an ugly or beautiful form are in flagrant opposition to the concept of the sutta on light and darkness and seem to also lack any sound basis in reality. The abstractions of the fool and the wise man began to lead their own lives here. The consequence could have been that persons passively accepted the state in which they found themselves.

### 5. *Gotama became Buddha by his aspiration and good karma*

The question was also asked why the ascetic Gotama could become the Buddha. What made it possible for him to reach enlightenment and

---

[12] Both groups of animals are considered a place of punishment for an evil-doer who formerly was enjoying objects of taste (*rasāda*).

release without the help of others and moreover[13] to help others to find the path (or paths) to salvation in such an impressive way? *Almost* all of the oldest transmissions of the Buddhist tradition concerning this point indicate that the exalted position of the Buddha could only be explained by the earnest wish to reach enlightenment and by good deeds during numerous former existences. This idea, too, presupposes that human intentions and actions are, to some extent, predetermined by past intentions and actions, but now in the positive sense of a spiritual development. The grounds for this optimistic view are that one thought that the consequences of good deeds could be converted to the development of a person by the earnest wish to become a Buddha and good karma was not consumed by enjoying worldly pleasures.

When I state "*almost* all of the oldest transmissions", then I am referring to a few fragments which are attributed to the school of the Mahāsaṅghikas. In these fragments (see Bareau *Les sectes* 57-61) it is stated that the Buddha always remains in (meditative) concentration. He never sleeps or dreams; he never speaks, but creatures think that he speaks and are joyous that he does. The body of the Buddha is infinite; his life is eternal and his power without end. This school could have explained the appearance of the Buddha as the manifestation of a supernatural principle. However, such a doctrine is attested only in Mahāyāna texts, the first document perhaps being the 15th chapter of the Saddharmapuṇḍarīkasūtra. For this reason I shall now return to the majority of the old transmissions and an explanation by means of the "natural" cause consisting in the undeviating effort directed towards enlightenment in numerous former existences. I want to restrict myself to the most relevant documents in the Pāli canon, the Jātakas and the Buddhavaṁsa.

The Jātakas are stories which are referred to the former lives of the Buddha. An animal, a man or a deity who plays a big or a small part in such a story is identified with a former existence of the Buddha. Very likely the nucleus of some of these stories already existed in the third cen-

[13] At some places in the Pāli canon (e.g. MN 116) persons called *paccekabuddha* are mentioned who have reached enlightenment without the help of others, but do not have the capacity to guide others. This category of persons can be understood as an attempt to do justice to ascetics of former times who were not dependent on the teaching of the Buddha, but nevertheless were held in high esteem. This group of persons seems to have been generally accepted in Buddhism, though with no great significance. It is said that these persons, who in Sanskrit are called *pratyekabuddha*, can be found in periods when no Buddha teaches and Buddhist doctrine is no longer known. M.A.G.Th. Kloppenborg described the most important aspects of this idea as it is found in the Theravāda tradition in *The Paccekabuddha, A Buddhist Ascetic*, Leiden 1974 (revised, Kandy 1983). See also J. Bronkhorst *The Two Traditions* p.120-121 (referring to M.G. Wiltshire's Ph.D. thesis, University of Lancaster 1980).

tury B.C.[14] Today the Pāli canon contains 547 stories in verses (the prose versions, which we often need to understand the verses, have not gained canonical status).

It is possible that these stories evolved from a kind of indirect admonition and also from a (sometimes amusing) instruction in worldly wisdom. Examples from the realm of animals and of the hoary past (partially copied from other traditions) show the immediate consequence of a certain behavior. The stories reflect disappointing experiences with fellow-beings, especially at a king's palace, but often also the wish to escape such a life and become an ascetic. The belief in later retribution of good and bad deeds is also present almost everywhere. Furthermore we often find the opinion that Sakka ( = Indra), who in most of these texts is the highest god (the first of the "Thirty-three"), master of a heaven of sensual pleasures, is forced to appear on earth and to intervene, when "his throne is heated" by extraordinary actions and intentions. Sometimes a result is achieved by an act of truth (*sacca-kiriyā*). If we look at the story of Aṅgulimāla in the first section of this chapter, *saccakiriyā* means stating an exceptional fact in such a way that at least one word bears an analogy with what one wants to achieve; it also means expressly appealing to the truth of that fact in order to realize one's wish.

The next step probably was the identification of figures in a story with persons in the company of the Buddha and with the Buddha himself in order to enliven homilies about tenets which in Vinaya- and Suttapiṭaka were transmitted in connection with the Buddha's praise and especially criticism of certain persons. The authority for the identification which follows a narration is said to be the Buddha's remembrance of his former existences. This is not without problems in regard to fables because the formula relating to this matter does not mention an existence in the realm of animals. The tenor of these identifications is that traits of character and relations between persons remain almost the same through many existences; a wicked intriguer is often identified with Devadatta, the Buddha's cousin who instigated a schism in the order.[15] The retribution of

[14] Cf. A. Bareau, The Place of the Buddha Gautama during the Reign of Asoka, *Festschrift Walpola Rahula*, 1-9. According to Bareau most Jātakas did not yet exist (as Buddhist stories) in the middle of the third century B.C. The compilation, revision and creation of these stories must have taken place in the two centuries after Asoka. As to archeological proof see Lamotte *Histoire* p.444, referring to H. Lüders, *Bhārhut und die buddhistische Literatur*, Leipzig 1941.

[15] The impression "once wicked, always wicked" is taken away in such stories as the Losaka Jātaka and Mahāsutasoma Jātaka in which all ends well in the present time; the wicked person in the second story is identified with Aṅgulimāla (the contents and interpretation of such stories can easily be found in G.P. Malalasekera's *Dictionary of Pāli Proper Names*, vol. I and II, [1937] reprinted London 1960). According to the Milindapañha (p. 111) there is also hope for Devadatta; at some time he will become a Paccekabuddha (cf. Saṅghabhedavastu Part II, ed. R. Gnoli p. 262).

karma becomes a protracted process which is not finished after one or two existences.

The third step probably was to demonstrate by means of such stories how Gotama could become a Buddha. This is not always convincing. In some tales the figure which is identified with the Bodhisattva[16] does nothing or nearly nothing (e.g. a deity who observes what happens and apparently is only introduced because one needed a figure which could be identified with Gotama in a former life) or acts in a clever, but morally questionable way or is only a skillful artisan. Other narratives are better suited for identification, e.g. where a king or a minister or a rich merchant gives away all his wealth and renounces the world. However one needed more impressive stories for this aim. We find narratives where the principal character sacrifices his own life, be it as a consequence of his care for others, be it deliberately. The latter happens when the hero wants te keep a vow or to cultivate some virtues to the extreme. These cases of deliberate sacrifice of one's life (or, in the famous story of Vessantara, the giving away of one's children and wife) are less serious than they seem at first sight. It is god Sakka who in almost all of these cases is challenged by the hero's resolution and wants to put him to the test (not to divert him out of jealousy as in other Indian tales). Afterwards Sakka repairs the damage caused by his provokation. In this sense Sakka is the most important assistent in the Bodhisattva's quest for enlightenment.

For an example we may take Jātaka no. 316[17]. Here the Bodhisattva is a hare and the moral guide of his friends, a monkey, a jackal and an otter. At a fast-day he advises them to collect food and give it to worthy persons. His friends all prepare some food. He himself has nothing but grass which cannot be given. He decides to offer his own body. Sakka [immediately] comes to know this decision (*saṅkappa*) and wants to put his liberality to the test. In the shape of a Brahman he approaches the hare. The hare says: I shall give you a gift which has never been given;

---

[16] Bodhisattva is a Sanskrit term to indicate a Buddha before his enlightenment (*bodhi*). It is possible that it is a wrong translation of the Middle Indic *bodhi-satta*, which perhaps originally meant *[a being] attached to , i.e. striving for, enlightenment* and in Sanskrit would be *bodhi-sakta*, and not *bodhi-sattva*, which suggests: *a being of, i.e. destined for, enlightenment* (see Har Dayal, *The Bodhisattva Doctrine in Buddhist Sanskrit literature*, [London 1932] Delhi 1978 p.7). *Sakta* was perhaps felt to be used too much in a negative sense, and moreover in legend the *bodhisatta* in his last life is more and more considered to be sure of his future enlightenment and not really having to strive for it. However the appearance of the word in probably old I-reports by Gotama about his vain efforts in the present existence (e.g. MN 4, I p.17) suggests "striving for enlightenment" as the original meaning.

[17] The canonical version consists of only four verses which do not give enough information. What follows is taken from Cariyāpiṭaka I 10. Cf. Malalasekera, op. cit., vol. II p.1078.

you are endowed with the virtue of ascetic conduct and are not allowed to kill another being; make a fire, I shall roast myself, then you can eat me. The fire being made he jumps into it, but by the power of Sakka it is like refreshing cool water.

After some time the Theravāda tradition of explaining the greatness of the Buddha by his deeds in former lives tried to adopt ideas developed in other Buddhist traditions where one thought that as many persons as possible should themselves become a Buddha and a series of perfections (*pāramī*) was commended. In the recension we now have of the Cariyāpiṭaka (a text which was not a canonical work for all Theravādins) the contents of 32 Jātakas (including their prose versions) and of three other stories[18] are outlined in order to show that Gotama had successively employed various perfections in his former existences. For each of the perfections of liberality (*dāna*) and ascetic conduct (*sīla*) ten good examples from the Jātakas are given. Instances of the perfections of patience (*khanti*) and of vigour (*viriya*) surely also occur, as the epilogue claims. But instances of the perfections of meditative concentration and of discriminating insight, even if this latter is not taken in a mahāyānistic sense, obviously could not be found[19], though, as we can see in MN 111 (III p.29 ... *pāramippatto* ... *samādhismiṁ* ... *pāramippatto* ... *paññāya*), the terminology was known and not disapproved. Instead one discovered some other perfections in the material of the Jātakas (and of other sources). In the third part of the Cariyāpiṭaka consisting of 15 stories the Bodhisattva is shown to have employed the perfections of renunciation (*nekkhama*), of resolution (*adhiṭṭhāna*), of truth (*sacca*), of friendliness (*mettā*) and of equanimity (*upekkhā*).

In the second chapter of the Buddhavaṁsa, which was not accepted by all Theravādins as a canonical book[20], it is related that many aeons ago Gotama, as the Brahman Sumedha, met the Buddha Dīpaṅkara and took the opportunity to honour him by covering a muddy part of the road on

---

[18] See K.R. Norman, *Pāli Literature*, Wiesbaden 1983, 31-35 and 94.

[19] Insight into the transiency of all things sometimes appears, but is only used as a motive for renunciation and the ascetic life (e.g. in the Yuvañjaya Jātaka, no. 460). In the second chapter of the Buddhavaṁsa (v.v. 116-164) ten perfections are mentioned: *dāna*, *sīla*, *nekkhama*, *paññā*, *viriya*, *khanti*, *sacca*, *adhiṭṭhāna*, *mettā* and *upekkhā* (without *samādhi* or *dhyāna*). What *paññā* means is not so clear. The same ten perfections appear in the Visuddhimagga (at the end of chapter 9), here *paññā* is only a means for discrimination of what is salutary (*hita*) to living beings and what not. So the question could not arise, as it did e.g. in the Aṣṭasāhasrikā-prajñāpāramitā-sūtra, how the Bodhisattva can employ a means which is known to immediately lead to nirvana and seems to leave no room for further development, i.e. becoming a Buddha (cf. T. Vetter, A Comparison ..., *Acta Indologica* VI, 1984, 506).

[20] See Malalasekera op.cit., vol.II p.310 and K.R. Norman op.cit., 31.

which Dīpaṅkara must pass with his hair and his clothes. He then expressed the wish to himself become a Buddha and attain omniscience on account of this meritorious act. By this service (*adhikāra*) and this wish expressed in Dīpaṅkara's presence (and perhaps also by Dīpaṅkara's prophesy that he will reach his goal) Sumedha's future lives were more and more directed towards this aim. It took aeons before this wish was fulfilled. If we look at the Jātakas, sometimes he went slightly off-course, but he saw his final harbour getting closer and closer. Good deeds enabled him to also do good and better deeds in the future. They improved his character and the capacity for heroic acts[21]. According to other chapters of the Buddhavaṁsa he visited and served each Buddha appearing in the meantime, thereby strengthening his aspiration and increasing his stock of merits.

The story in the Buddhavaṁsa takes for granted that there were Buddhas in other aeons. This idea does not play a role in the ancient canonical literature used in the previous chapters. In Asoka's time (3rd cen. B.C.) certainly two predecessors of Gotama were honoured, Konāgamana and Kassapa.[22] In the Mahāpadāna sutta, which does not

---

[21] The best explanation of the connection between good deeds and the improvement of character seems to be the Sanskrit word *pariṇāmayati* as it is used in Mahāyāna texts: devoting good karma to a goal that not automatically originates from it, especially enlightenment, even of others ("transference of merit"). See L. Schmithausen, Der Nirvāṇa-Abschnitt in der Viniścayasaṃgrahaṇī der Yogācārabhūmiḥ, Wien 1969, p. 165.

An example of some slight influence on the result of karma (but only on some possibilities of its external reward, not on another goal) can be found in AN 8.4.5. Someone gives gifts to ascetics and brahmans and he gives willingly. He wishes to be reborn in a future existence amongst wealthy warriors or wealthy Brahmans or wealthy citizens, or in the heaven of the four great kings, or among the thirty-three gods, or among the Yāma gods, or among the Tusita gods, or among the Nimmānarati gods, or among the Paranimmitavasavatti gods, or among the Brahmakāyika gods. He thinks constantly (*bhāveti*) of one of these places. If he is someone who follows the rules of ascetic conduct (as far as is possible in the life of a householder; cf. MN 120), then the earnest wish (*paṇidhi*) of his heart will be fulfilled because he is [morally] pure (*ijjhati* ... *sīlavato cetopaṇidhi visuddhatā*). In later times an earnest wish is assumed to do more with good karma than only make such a choice between possibilities that could anyway result from one's karma. But sometimes reaching a "heavenly" place such as Sukhāvatī by one's earnest wish and directing one's karma to this goal can remain an important stage on the way to enlightenment and nirvana (cf. Sukhāvatīvyūha in *Mahāyānasūtrasaṃgraha* ed. Vaidya, Darbhanga 1961, 241: *ye ... sattvās ... bahv aparimitaṃ kuśalamūlam avaropayiṣyanti bodhaye cittaṃ pariṇāmya tatra ca lokadhātāv upapattaye praṇidhāsyanti, ... ... / ... ... / ... tasmin buddhakṣetre cittaṃ sampreṣya upapattaye kuśalamūlāni ca pariṇāmayitavyāni*. The connection between earnest wish (*praṇidhi*), devoting [one's good karma] or directing [one's mind with its potential of good karma] (*pariṇāmayati*) and rebirth (*upapatti*) can also be found in the Mahākarmavibhaṅga in the same volume edited by Vaidya p. 189 (in the edition of S. Lévi p. 50).

[22] See Bareau op.cit. (in note 14), p.6.

seem to be composed before Asoka, the names and some peculiarities of six of Gotama's predecessors are mentioned (DN 14, II p.5), Vipassin, Sikhin, Vessabhu, Kakusandha, Konāgamana and Kassapa. Later the Buddhavaṁsa lists 24 predecessors, the 24th Buddha before Gotama was Dīpaṅkara. In DN 26 (III p.76) Metteyya is mentioned as Gotama's successor.[23]

In this context the Mahāpadāna sutta introduces a new source of knowledge which transcends the remembrance of former lives and the observation of the disappearance and rebirth of other beings. The Tathāgata knows details of the lives of former Buddhas, because he penetrates the essence of things (*dhammadhātu*, DN II p.10). It is the nature of things (*dhammatā*, DN II p.12) that when a Bodhisattva, i.e. Vipassin and the other Buddhas before their enlightenment, descends from the Tusita heaven into his mother's womb, an immeasurable light appears in the world, and that when he has entered his mother's womb four deities come to protect him, etc., etc. (cf. MN 123).

---

[23] More details can be found in R. Gombrich, The Significance of Former Buddhas in the Theravādin Tradition, in Festschrift for Walpola Rahula, p. 64-72.

APPENDIX

# MYSTICISM IN THE AṬṬHAKAVAGGA

The Aṭṭhakavagga, or for short Aṭṭhaka, is the only part of the Suttanipāta which as such can be found in the Chinese Tripiṭaka (T.198).

In the Pāli Udāna (V 6) it is said to be recited in sixteen sections. The same sentence occurs in Vinaya I (p.198); here, however, without the word "sixteen". The name Aṭṭhaka for the fourth part of the Pāli Suttanipāta probably derives from the fact that four of its sixteen suttas (no.2 up to no.5) consist of "eight" *tuṭṭubha*-verses. This would point to a very superficial criterion at the start of collecting these suttas.

On the other hand, the sixteen suttas we now have before us (arranged according to the increasing number of verses, as R. Gombrich observed) have some peculiar traits in common, e.g. scarcely a trace of the method of discriminating insight (i.e. judging the constituents as non-self), and some of them, which I call the nucleus of the Aṭṭhaka, lack approval, to put it mildly, of any issue proclaimed at other places as being essential for Buddhism.

Here, obviously, material has not been taken from everywhere to reach the solemn number of sixteen suttas. As I shall try to demonstrate, the Aṭṭhaka probably contains texts of a group that existed before or alongside the first Buddhist teaching and community. After some time this circle was integrated into the Buddhist Saṅgha. Then it produced more texts. In these texts it tried to combine its old teaching with the teaching of the Buddha, taking from the latter what seemed suitable and often, but not always, losing its initial radicalness.

There are metrical arguments against the original unity of the Aṭṭhaka which I cannot discuss here. I made use of them when they were confirmed by observations of the contents.

In order to determine the uniformity and diversity of the contents I shall start with the main contention of the article "Proto-Mādhyamika in the Pāli canon" by Louis O. Gomez (*Philosophy East and West* 1976, 137-165). According to Gomez, in the Aṭṭhaka (and also in the Pārāyana) there are passages implying a mystic state and a way to it that, being comparable only to later developments such as in Mādhyamika and in Zen, cannot be reduced to other, more common teachings of the Pāli canon. I agree with this interpretation, but want to add some historical refinement to it.

We can use this interpretation for determining the contents of the suttas of the Aṭṭhaka, because not all of them show this goal or recommend a way to it, and of those that contain these issues some have them in a form mixed up with other, less compatible, tenets. I shall, therefore, not ascribe this mysticism to *the* Aṭṭhaka (or *the* Pārāyana) as Gomez does.

This mysticism has in common with Mādhyamika and Zen an extreme apophatic tendency which (in the words of Gomez, 140) "could be characterized in the theoretical realm as the doctrine of no-views, and in the practical realm as the practice of practicing no dharmas. In its extreme manifestations this tendency is diametrically opposed to the doctrine of right-views and the practice of gradually and systematically cultivating the true or pure dharmas".

To support this contention Gomez cites passages that advise overcoming or denying apperception (*saññā*), knowledge, views, learning, thoughts, ascetic morality and vows. I shall critically discuss some of these passages. But even if we suppose, for the moment, that all these passages can be accepted as proof without reservation, then there remain six out of the sixteen suttas of the Aṭṭhaka that are not used by Gomez for his argument, and could not be used, because they do not have instances required for this case. These suttas are the Kāma, the Guhaṭṭhaka, the Duṭṭhaṭṭhaka, the Jarā, the Tissametteya and the Sāriputta Sutta. In this connection I may mention that the Kāma, the Guhaṭṭhaka and the Jarā Sutta give the impression of not being so old when looked at from the angle of metrics.

There are also passages cited by Gomez which are problematic. I will not discuss the problems here and only make some general remarks on the suttas from which these citations are taken. The Tuvaṭaka bears some traces (916-919) of the topic under discussion, but has adapted this teaching and is only an adulterated authority in this matter. The Attadaṇḍa has only one sentence (954) which is slightly reminiscent of our subject. The Purābheda, too, has some traces (856) of our theme, but also some statements that complicate the matter (see below).

There remain seven suttas of the Aṭṭhaka which are a good basis for Gomez' contention. Omitting some observations on the opposition between Brahmanas and Samanas in these suttas (in fact they are suttas of Brahmanas, one of which accepting *the* Samaṇa [the Buddha]), let us now take a brief look at their contents.

The Pasūra-sutta mainly advocates an abstention from disputes and appears only to express a peace of noninvolvement. But the two concluding verses are capable of being interpreted as integrating these thoughts into a way to a higher peace (Gomez 146). We may also take into account that this sutta has been included between other suttas proclaiming such a higher peace.

But how can we become more sure of such a higher goal? There are two fairly plausible arguments. Some of these suttas, while (with one exception) also recommending abstention from disputes, criticize clinging to apperception (*saññā*), and some of these suttas describe the method to reach the higher peace by a special middle path (not the same middle path we know from the Buddha's first preaching).

I shall skip some passages relating to the advice on overcoming apperception; some of them are not very convincing proof for a kind of mysticism.

A better manner to show this is to find instances of a middle path, i.e. passages where not only all dogmas are denied and all theories and knowledge (which could be interpreted as merely aiming at a peace of noninvolvement) and all apperceptions (which is a stronger argument), but where this denying itself is denied. With such a double denying one can avoid the impression that the mental state one aims for is similar to the state of a stone or plant which apparently have no apperceptions. One can imagine some criticism on this point; such a middle path would, then, be a development in the teaching.

The best instance is verse 874 in the Kalahavivāda-sutta. In the translation of Gomez(144) this difficult verse reads: "When he has not an apperception of apperceptions (*na saññasaññī*), when he has not an apperception of non-apperception (*na visaññasaññī*), when he does not not apperceive (*no pi asaññī*), when he does not have apperceptions without an object (*na vibhūtasaññī*), for him who has attained to this, form ceases, for apperception is the cause of dispersion and conception (*papañca-saṅkhā*, probably better: conception of dispersion)."

We may add that, according to a question in 873, for such a person not only form (*rūpa*) ceases, but also pleasure and pain. Looking at 872 we may also say "name and form" (*nāma-rūpa*) ceases. Contrary to *nāma-rūpa* being conditioned by *viññāṇa* (and its conditions) in the twelvefold chain of dependent origination, here *nāma-rūpa* seems to be dependent on *saññā* and ceases in this very life (we may interpret: does not appear for a while), and not only (and definitely) after death. That these verses, and the whole sutta, are directed against the structure at the beginning of the twelvefold chain cannot be excluded merely because they contain thoughts one is not used to, which has induced scholars to consider this sutta the origin of all attempts to construe chains of dependence. I think that this sutta represents a later stage in the development of the teaching of this mysticism. I shall point below to a hardly dubitable example of criticism of an advanced Buddhist term.

Another example of such a middle path can be found in the Māgaṇḍiya-sutta. Gomez (p. 146) translates: "Cleansing is not attained by things seen or heard (...*diṭṭhiyā* ... *sutiyā*, better: by views or learning), nor by knowledge, nor by the vows of morality (*sīlabbatena*, better: by morals and vows, see line 4), nor is it attained by not seeing or not hearing, nor by not knowing, nor by absence of morals and vows. Abandoning all these, not grasping at them he is at peace; not relying he would not hanker for becoming'' (839).

The beginning lines of this verse imply that the goal is not reached by persons who never think and have learned nothing and have no ascetic conduct, but thinking etc., apparently must be left behind at some moment. Perhaps we may also conclude that this goal, if it is reached by overcoming all apperceptions, as the last verse of this sutta strongly suggests (847 [Gomez p.145]: ''For him who is detached from apperceptions there are no knots. ...''), is not under, but above all apperceptions.

I now want to leave the theme of mysticism and to look at these seven suttas of the Aṭṭhaka from the angle of release from rebirth, so conspicuous a theme in the Pārāyana. Only with difficulty can one find some passages that perhaps recommend this goal. There is, however, much criticism of the striving for purity as a means for better rebirth. ''Real purity'' is: not to strive for anything, surely not for this or that existence.

One might expect that also striving for non-becoming would be criticized. With one exception, at the end of the Kalahavivāda, this cannot be found in the seven suttas. In the Purābheda-sutta we see, however, a clear rejection of striving for both becoming and non-becoming. The Purābheda-sutta shows some ''Buddhist'' influence (Gotama is mentioned in 848 and the fourth dhyāna is alluded to in 855), but has much in common with the suttas under discussion.

We can perhaps explain this observation. In the oldest days this movement was only confronted by groups of persons who strove for a better existence after this life, not groups of persons who strove for release from rebirth. At some moment this latter goal, being not too far from renouncing any effort striving for better existences, was heard of and recognized by these mystics, but nevertheless they rejected striving for it. With this explanation we can perhaps understand the third part of the tripartition of craving found in the Pāli tradition of the four noble truths. The craving for *vibhava* (''non-becoming'') may be an addition to the four noble truths, coming from the, now, Buddhist circle where the Purābheda-sutta was composed.

If we use a Buddhist term, occurring only twice in the Aṭṭhaka (and not in the nucleus), we could say: in this circle the *nibbāna* is conceived as complete extinction of all desires, even of the desire for release from rebirth. The second meaning of *nibbāna*, extinction of rebirth, would, by the way, presuppose a theory or view about rebirth, whereas all theories, as we heard, are to be rejected.

An instance of openly rejecting this second meaning of nibbāna seems to be extant at the end of the Kalahavivāda, where experts who proclaim *anupādisesa* are criticized. I see no other manner to understand this *anupādisesa* than to interpret it in the traditional way as release where no psychic and material "possessions" remain.

If I am right in this interpretation, we have to admit that such a critical remark about a widely accepted Buddhist goal could only be made some time after the first events and teachings we gather from the Buddha's biography. But because the Kalahavivāda, having a middle path formulation, is one of the most advanced of the seven "non-Buddhist" suttas of the Aṭṭhaka, there are no obstacles to the assumption that the origin of this movement lay before (the knowledge of) the preaching of the Buddha.

The goal of overcoming all apperceptions seems not to be in conflict with the genuine dhyāna meditation, though dhyāna tolerates or even presupposes right views and ascetic morality and such things. So we can understand that this group of mystics could be integrated into the Gotama-saṅgha and tried to adapt specific Buddhist methods (e.g. mindfulness) and aims as is the case in other suttas of the Aṭṭhaka. On the other hand, the Gotama-saṅgha attempted to include (mainly in the sense of Paul Hacker's term "inclusivism") the main subject of this movement or to make use of it (e.g. to reject all theories, when, in the development of the paññā stream, questions as the (non-)annihilation of a released person presented too many difficulties, cf. Sn 1076, MN 72 [see chapter 11]).

The first attempts to include this theme may be found in the Pārāyana. In the Upasīva and Nanda sections "inclusion" comes near to acceptance, but in the Upasīva section overcoming apperception is supported by mindfulness, and in the Nanda section the method of overcoming all views and knowledge is explicitly employed for the aim of release from birth and old age and is combined with "knowing" craving. In the Posāla section, however, we meet an example of blank "inclusivism". What is called in the Upasīva section "emancipation from apperception" is here only a state of nothingness, which could be a fetter (1115), and has to be overcome by knowledge.

This reminds us of the state of nothingness as one of the four states in the realm without forms (see chapter 12) and the appreciation, common in Buddhism, of this state and the rest of these states as not leading to release from rebirth. Gomez (note 45) may be right, when he says that we must not reduce the state described in verse 874, which resembles the state of neither apperception nor non-apperception, to a meditational state of the realm without forms. But even in early times Buddhists thought they could do this, the starting point being perhaps (or registered by) the Posāla-section of the Pārāyana. And from their point of view they were right; this state of mind was not originally intended to overcome rebirth. They were, however, not right in supposing that this state of mind, which in the meantime had been called cessation of apperceptions and feelings, was intended for less than their goal; for these mystics considered themselves standing above the question of rebirth or no rebirth. When they became integrated into the Gotama-saṅgha, they could, with a good conscience, maintain that they, too, were released from rebirth. But to convince the other side it was necessary to show that by such a state of mind the faults which according to the other side's view cause rebirth were destroyed. However, what the opponents expected as a means was not implied. It may be that this problem led to the strange formulation "staying in the cessation of apperceptions and feelings, his cankers have completely vanished after having seen by *paññā*". As Schmithausen (1981, note 55) has observed this passage is missing in Dīgha-nikāya and Samyutta-nikāya. This may prove that the monks specializing in these Nikāyas had a good sense of dogmatics, though not of mysticism.

# INDEX


Abhidharmakośa(bhāṣya) XVIII, 15 n.4, 43 n.12, 48, 50, 52 + n.9, 55, 72 n.2 + 3, 83 n.5, 84 n.6, 88 n.3, 92 n.9
*abyākata* 55
Akaniṣṭha gods 72 n.2
Ajita Kesakambala 12 n.4, 77, 78, 84
*anāgāmin* 16 n.5, *70*
Ānanda XI, XII, XV, 41 n.11
*ananta* 44
*ānantarya-karma* 88
Anattapariyāya 35-41
Aṅgulimāla 89-90, 96 n.15
Aṅguttara Nikāya (no. 8.1.8) VIII, (8.11 = 8.2.1) XXIV n.8, (9.4.8) 6, (7.5.2) 11 n.1, (10.17.10) 12 n.4, (10.11.3) 13 n.5, (8.7.4) 19 n.4, (8.7.3) 26, (9.1.5) 35 n.2, (3.8.6) 50, (6.6.9) 52, (10.3.5) 66, (10.1.6-7 and 11.1.7-9) 66 n.5, (6.6.6) 67 n.8, (6.5.4) 68 n.9, (10.17.11) 83 n.5, (6.6.9) 84 and 88 n.2, (10.21.7-9) 90-91, (4.24.2) 90 n.5, (4.9.7; 5.11.4; 10.6.10) 91, (3.10.9) 91 n.6, (8.4.5) 99
animals 83, 84, 93-94, 95
apperception (*saññā*) 36 + n.4, 37, 64, 65 n.2, 68 n.10, 102-106
Ārāḍa Kālāma XXII, 67 n.7
Aramaki, N. XII n.5
*arhat* *8 n.3*, 70, 88 + n.3, 89
*arūpa-dhātu*, *ārūpya-dhātu* 72
ascetic conduct XXIII, XXXV, XXXVI
asceticism, rules (or prescriptions) of a. XII, XXV, *22*, 85
ascetics, the five a. XXVIII, 8, 10, 45

Bareau, A. IX, XI n.4, XIII, XIV n.8, XIX, XXI, XXII, 3 n.1, 7 n.1, 8, 17, 67 n.7, 81 n.3, 83 n.5, 89 n.4, 92 n.11, 95, 96 n.14, 99 n.22
Basham, A. L. 15 n.4
Bechert, H. XIII n.7, XIV, XVIII n.2
Beckh, H. XV, 21 n.6
Bernhard, F. 46 n.2
bodhisattva 97 + n.16, 98
Brahma heaven 27, 84 n.6
Brahmanas and Samaṇas 102
Bronkhorst, J. IX, XIX, XXII, 3 n.1 + 3, 67 n.6 + 7, 95 n.13
Buddha, biographical data on the B. XI-XIV; legend XIV-XV; his enlightenment XXVIII, XXXII, XXXIII, chapter five; his former lives as a bodhisattva 94-99; other buddhas 99-100
Buddhaghosa, see Visuddhimagga
Buddhavaṁsa 95, 98-99

cankers (*āsava*, *āsrava*) XXIV, chapter eight, 38 n.6, 40, 45, 63, 106
Cariyāpiṭaka 97 n.17, 98
Casparis, J. G. de 15 n.4
cessation of apperceptions and feelings (*saññāvedayita-nirodha*) XXI, XXXVI, 63, 64, *67-71*, 106
*cetovimutti* XXXII, XXXV, 26, 63, 67 n.8
Collins, S. 43 n.12
confession and repentance of bad deeds 87 + n.1
constituents of a person XXXIV, XXXV, 14 n.2, 36, 50, 58
craving (*taṇhā*, *tṛṣṇā*) XXI, XXV, 14 n.4, 15, 45, 46, 47, 48, 51, 104

*dāna* 85, 98
Dayal, H. 97 n.16
Demiéville, P. 82 n.4
Devadatta VIII, XI, XII, 88 n.3, 92, 96 + n.15
*dhamma*, *dharma* XI, 9 n.4, 21, 23, 45
Dhamma-cakka-ppavattana-sutta XXVIII, XXXIV, chapter two, 14, 17, 35
*dhamma-dhātu* 100
Dhammadinnā XXXVI, 13
*dhammatā* 100
Dharmaguptakas 8, 17, 18, 19
Dharmakīrti, see Pramāṇavārttika
dhyāna-meditation XXI, XXIII, XXV-XXVI, XXVI n.9, XXIX, chapter one, 10, 27, 35, 104
Dīgha Nikāya (no.2) XXXVII, (2) 12 n.4, (11) 44, (1) 49, (14) 49 n.4, (1;2) 55, 65 n.3, (16) 67 n.8, (16) 68, (9) 68 n.10, (2) 78, (1) 79, (1) 81 n.3, (31) 85 n.7, (5) 85 n.8, (2) 87 n.1, (33) 90 n.5, (16) 92, (14) 99-100, (2) 100, 106
Dīpaṅkara 98-99
discriminating insight (*paññā*, *prajñā*) XII, XXII, XXIII, XXXIV-XXXVI,

Makkhali Gosāla 78-79
Malalasekera, G.P. 96 n.15, 97 n.17, 98 n.20
Māra 6, 49
Maudgalyāyana, Mogallāna XI, XII, 45
McDermott, J.P. 92 n.11
Meisig K. XXVI n.9, 87 n.1
middle way XXVIII, 7, *9-10*, 55, 59, 103
Milindapañha XVIII, 78, 92 + n.10 + 11, 96 n.15
Mūlasarvāstivāda-vinaya (Saṅghabheda-vastu) XXXIII, 7 n.1, 8, 10 n.8, 17, 18, 35 n.2, 36, 39 n.8, 40, 96 n.15

Nakamura, H. XIII n.7
name and form 46, 48, 49, 59, 103
nimitta 67 n.8
nirvana (P. *nibbāna*) XIII, XIV, XVI, 9 n.6, *15-16*, 43, 70, *71*, 104
non-self XXII, XXXIV, XXXV, 35, 36, 39 + n.8, 41-44
Norman, K.R. XVII n.1, XXIX n.10, 9 n.6, 14 n.1, 31 n.3, 98 n.18 + 20
nothingness 63, 64, 105
Nyanatiloka XXXVI n.11, 13, 92 + n.10
Nyāya 43 n.12

obstacles, five o. 25
Oldenberg, H. XVIII
Oort, M. IX
order (*saṅgha*) XI, XXXIV, 10 n.8, 101, 105, 106
origination, twelvefold chain of dependent o. (*paṭicca-samuppāda*, *pratītya-samutpāda*) 31, chapter ten, 54, 58, 59, 60

*paccekabuddha*, *pratyekabuddha* 95 n.13, 96 n.15
Pāli XVIII
*paññā-vimutti* XXXV, 26 n.2, 63
Pannenberg, W. VIII
*pariṇāmayati* 99 n.21
path, noble eightfold p. XXVIII, XXX, XXXVII, chapter three, 15, 21; dhyāna p., chapter six
*paṭicca-samuppanna* 38
perception (*viññāṇa*, *vijñāna*) 36 + n.4, 37, 44, 46, *48-50*, 54, 59; infinity of p. 64-65, 103
Pérez-Remón, J. 39 n.8, 41 n.10
perfection (*pāramī*, *pāramitā*) XXXV, 98 + n.19
Pramāṇavārttika 15 n.4, 43 n.12, 44 n.13
*pudgala* 42-43

rebirth XVI, XXI, XXIII, 14, 29, 47, 48-49, 78, 79, 90 + n.5, 104
release from rebirth and suffering passim
*rūpa-dhātu* 72 + n.1, 84 n.6

*sacca-kiriyā* [89], 96
Saddharmapuṇḍarīkasūtra 95
Sakka (Indra) 83 n.6, 96, 97
Śālistamba-sūtra 50
salvation, the expression "to seek s." XV-XVI
*samādhi* XXV, XXVI n.9, XXXIII, 5, 10, 13, 26, 27
Saṃyutta Nikāya (no.2.12) 6, (56.11) 7 n.1, (38.1) 15-16, (2.22) 23 n.3, (44.10) 41 n.11, (35.106) 48, (4.23) 49, (12.67) 49 n.4, (22.85) 57 n.3, (12.17) 58, (12.67) 59, (18.9) 65, (55.21) 65 n.3, (6.15) 68, (3.21) 79-80, (8.7) 82 n.4, (7.19; 1.47; 1.32) 85, (36.21) 91-92, 106
Sañjaya Belaṭṭhiputta 55
Śāriputra, Sāriputta XI, 15, 38 + n.6, 45, 57 n.3, 59, 69
Sarvāstivādins XXXV, 15 n.4
*sassata* 58
*sati* XXV, XXVI n.9, 22, *24*, [105]
*satipaṭṭhāna* 26 n.1
Sautrāntikas 52 n.9
Schmithausen, L. IX, XVIII, XIX, XXI, XXIII, XXIV, XXXVI n.11, 21 n.1, 31 n.2, 35 n.1, 36 n.3 + 4, 37 n.5, 40 n.9, 41 n.11, 65 n.2, 70 n.11, 71 n.12, 81 n.3, 90 n.5, 99 n.21, 106
Schneider, U. XV
Schopen, G. IX, 88 n.1
Schrader, F.O. 57 n.2
"second sermon" XXXIV, 10 n.8, see Anattapariyāya
self-mortification XXIII, XXVIII, XXIX, 4
sphere-meditation, chapter 12
Sthaviras XIV
*subhāsita* VIII
suffering 14, 40, passim; the origin of s. XXI, 14, chapter 10
Sukhāvatīvyūha 35 n.2, 99 n.21
*suñña* 38
supersession of evil karma 88 n.1
*sūtra* VIII
*sutta* VIII
sutta on light and darkness (SN 3.21) 79-80
Sutta-piṭaka VIII, XVII
Suttanipāta VII, (v.1107) XXVI n.9, (1109) 15, (1094) 16, (1086-87) 16, (Dvayatānupassanāsutta)16 n.5, (v.881)